THE NEW SAGA LIBRARY
GENERAL EDITOR: HERMANN PÁLSSON

Hrolf Gautreksson

A VIKING ROMANCE

HROLF
GAUTREKSSON

a Viking Romance

TRANSLATED BY HERMANN PÁLSSON

AND PAUL EDWARDS

University
of Toronto
Press

1972

,ISHERS) LTD
ardens
Edinburgh E H 9 I N R

UNESCO
COLLECTION OF REPRESENTATIVE WORKS
ICELANDIC SERIES
This work has been accepted in the Icelandic Translations
series of the United Nations Educational, Scientific, and
Cultural Organization (UNESCO).

First published in Great Britain
by Southside (Publishers) Ltd
Edinburgh 1972

Hardback S.B.N. 900025-01-8
Paperback S.B.N. 900025-02-6

First published in Canada and the United States
by University of Toronto Press
Toronto and Buffalo 1972

Hardback I.S.B.N. 0-8020-1814-9
Microfiche I.S.B.N. 0-8020-0138-6

Copyright © Introduction & Translation
Hermann Pálsson & Paul Edwards 1972

Printed in Great Britain
by Neill & Co. Ltd
212 Causewayside
Edinburgh E H 9 I P P
Scotland

Contents

Introduction

ONE OF THE MOST CHARACTERISTIC FEATURES of medieval Icelandic legendary fiction is the manner in which unrelated, and even incongruous, elements are at times fused together, creating a situation which can only be accepted at a literary level. Because of this, even though the legendary tales may contain historical elements, they are unacceptable as history. The English title we have given this translation attempts to make this point, in that it reflects two of the different levels at which the tale is conceived. At one level it is a story about a group of legendary Scandinavian figures pursuing lives in some respects similar to those of the vikings during the period A.D. 800 to 1000 (though the record of this viking life is highly stylised and idealised as it appears in the story). The heroes of the tale venture out again and again on expeditions, to conquer land or to capture loot and longships, making themselves famous or infamous and picking up a number of women on the way: but at another level the story refers to a later and more refined period, the Age of Chivalry with its courtly manners, its decadent wealth, its life of leisure and luxury, jousting and knightly pursuits. The hero may start life in the acquisitive and ambitious viking tradition, but sooner or later he betrays his affinities with the heroes of Romance. Some of the heroes of the Icelandic legendary tales would have been reasonably at home in the court of King Arthur at Camelot, and indeed these tales fuse elements in a way not at all unlike those of

7

Arthur, whose barbarous origins in Celtic myth and legend can be traced through the *Mabinogion* or Geoffrey of Monmouth to appear largely though not totally transformed in the knightly Christian king of Malory. But Hrolf Gautreksson has no Round Table, and many of the literary conventions of the tale are of native Icelandic origin in spite of the Romance varnish which glosses over some of the more barbaric elements.

Hrolf Gautreksson[1] is a story of action and change. The central heroic figure is a fighting man who travels from land to land in search of wealth and women: during the course of the narrative kingdoms crumble, new ones are created, sometimes bringing new attitudes but usually involving a return to the old viking way after a period of comparative peace – all this a reflexion of the turbulence of the Viking Age, still remembered, though imperfectly, centuries later. The scene shifts from one end of the viking world to the other, from Russia and the Baltic in the east to England and Ireland in the west. But whereas the true vikings went out in search of wealth, land, and power, the heroes of *Hrolf Gautreksson* undertake long expeditions in pursuit of that persistent object of Romance, the hand of a reluctant or inaccessible lady. So the romantic element softens the harsh surfaces of an otherwise masculine narrative, introducing emotional features which can transform the barbaric hero almost, at times, into the perfect gentleman. Yet there is in this

---

1. The present translation is based on the edition in Guðni Jónsson's Fornaldarsögur Norðurlanda (1950), IV. 53–176.

tale little of the romantic, as distinct from the Romance,[2] love which gave *Gunnlaug's Saga* and *Laxdæla Saga* such a powerful appeal to novel readers of the past century. While the women of *Hrolf Gautreksson* are usually made of sterner stuff than Helga the Fair, their passions are far removed from those of a Gudrun Osvif's daughter. For instance, Thornbjorg, whom the hero of the tale wins after a long hard struggle, is an amazon who combines knightly with more feminine skills, moving with confidence, after her marriage to Hrolf Gautreksson, between the boudoir and the battlefield. She bears an obvious resemblance to the great valkyrie-type heroines of the Eddic poetry, but is at the same time a much more flexible personality, in human terms, than Brynhild or Gudrun of the Edda. Thornbjorg's submission to her husband is complete, and her virginal past precludes a tragedy of the Nibelungen type. Emotional complexities do not belong here, and the story is not concerned with love triangles: warfare, heroism, an endless search for fame and riches, these are the principal ingredients of the tale, and it is through these exploits that its central themes are explored. This is an adventure story, at least at a surface level, where the motivation is provided by the incessant urge of one character or another to acquire something beyond

---

2. It may here be useful to stress the difference between *romantic* love, of a personal and passionate kind, and the *Romance* love of this tale, which is likely to strike the modern reader as a very much more formal affair.

his reach. The tension of the tale is artfully sustained by the gulf between the attainability of the desired object on one hand, and the limited resources of the seeker on the other, while the form of the tale is achieved by shifts of perspective into what are basically similar episodes of conquest and courtship. The hero must always fight against heavy odds, but that neither deters him from trying nor stops him from winning. The adventure story is essentially not tragic, and the happy outcome is as inevitable as the severity of the tests to which the heroes are subjected.

We might say, then, that *Hrolf Gautreksson*, like many of the legendary sagas, conflates material of three principal kinds. At one level is the ancient legendary material, in which nature and natural processes are constantly being distorted. This is a world of sorcery, giants, dwarfs, magic swords, and prophetic horns. At another level there is the viking material with certain codes of conduct (not always observed – there are good and bad vikings), plenty of physical action and violence, heroic exploits in search of loot, fine weapons, good ships, land, and a reputation for courage rather than courtesy: it reflects an age of energetic acquisitiveness. And at a third level we have material from the period of literary Romance, where emphasis is laid on courtly manners and self-control superimposed on the older virtues of courage and ambition. Filtering through from European Romance come ideas about how food should be cooked (here, as in *Arrow Odd*,[3] another of the same *genre*, a

---

3. See *Arrow-Odd: A Medieval Novel*, tr. H. Pálsson & P. Edwards, New York (U.P.) 1970, p. 27.

mark of a bad viking is that he eats raw meat), how it should be eaten in polite company, how ladies should conduct themselves in the boudoir, how the hero should engage on a marriage-quest: a world of heroic chivalry, courtesy and magnanimity. Yet it must be pointed out that none of these levels reflects a life ever known directly by the story teller or his public, for this is essentially escape literature. The interest in a leisured life reflects not a prosperous period in Iceland, but a mode of fantasy-escapism in a period of increasing economic strain and political mediocrity, with the loss of independence in 1262, and the subsequent economic burdens laid on the country.

YET DESPITE THESE BLURRING FACTORS, certain clear lines of theme and narrative emerge from the tale, which is concerned principally with two sets of personal relationships, those of marriage and those of blood-brotherhood.

Explored through these relationships is the central moral theme of excess and moderation. Four times in the tale a man sets out on a marriage-quest, aided by or on behalf of a blood-brother, and each quest examines conduct and responsibility in a slightly different light.

Though the tale is largely concerned with the lives of young and vigorous men, it opens on a quiet note with the hero's father, the aging King Gautrek,[4] lamenting the death of his

---

4. For Gautrek's earlier adventures and those of his father Gauti, see *Gautrek's Saga and other Medieval Tales*, tr. H. Pálsson & P. Edwards, London (U.L.P.) and New York (U.P.) 1968.

queen, and with Hrolf Gautreksson himself as yet unborn. Gautrek's lack of an heir and his negative conduct over his wife's death are seen by the court as unreasonable and politically dangerous. The courtiers suggest a new marriage, but since they do so with proper courtesy and respect, moderation is seen to beget moderation:

> King Gautrek took the suggestion in good part and said they were showing him the same goodwill now that they'd always shown by giving him their advice and their loyal support.

So he goes off in search of a young wife. Now the girl he proposes to marry has to make a choice between a handsome young suitor, as yet untested but with good prospects, and the elderly Gautrek. Far from acting on what would appear a natural and passionate impulse by choosing the younger man, the girl applies her reason to the situation and expresses her decision in words both moderate and courteous. She is to be the first of a series of 'wise counsellors,' many of them women, who recommend the controlled rather than the impassioned choice to the unvarying advantage of those who decide to take their advice. This is a world in which stability is preserved very much by way of 'common sense' and social forms. The girl, Ingibjorg, confronts her two suitors, and her father opens the discussion with a reasoned statement of the problem, inviting the girl to decide the issue for herself. The whole episode is conducted with a good deal of formality, and great importance is placed upon courtesy and polite conduct: here are Ingibjorg's concluding remarks:

. . . 'As I see it, this is far too delicate a problem for me to handle sensibly, or for any other woman with as little experience as I have; and it's far from certain that I'd make the best choice for myself. I think it's quite clear that both kings are very great men and more than good enough for me, whichever of them ultimately looks after me. But bearing in mind certain precedents, this is the conclusion I've come to: these two kings might be compared with two apple-trees standing in the same orchard. One is young and promises to yield a fine crop of big, sweet-tasting apples before reaching the full ripeness of his life; that's the tree that stands for King Olaf. Besides this, there's another apple-tree with lots of branches, heavy with all kinds of apples: that tree stands for King Gautrek's authority and power, for his long reign has been marked by his generosity and distinction, and now his kingdom is in full flower. We all know how brave and open-handed he is, and if his reign were to be cut short by natural causes, even so, perhaps he could still beget sturdy sons to make up for the loss. So although Olaf is the younger man, and likely to make a splendid king, to pay for a promise is always a risky bargain. I'm not going to elaborate on this any further just now, but the one I choose is King Gautrek, to live with and to enjoy. Even if I knew for certain that he'd only live for a few years, and that Olaf was fated to grow as old as a stone bridge, I've a feeling he could never be as great a king as Gautrek, and certainly not if Olaf hasn't all that long to live.'

Gautrek is delighted, of course: but Olaf is furious, and when his army intercepts Gautrek's on the way home, he challenges Gautrek to a fight. Gautrek proves the wisdom of the girl's choice and justifies the implied prophecy of her last sentence by slicing his way like a young warrior through Olaf's army and killing him.

But the second marriage-quest develops rather differently. Hrolf, son of Gautrek and Ingibjorg, is the suitor this time, but the girl, Thornbjorg, acts with unreasonable aggressiveness, rejecting one suitor after another with mockery and even violence. She refuses to allow herself to be addressed as a woman, treats her father with thinly veiled contempt, insists on being called king in her own right, dresses in armour like a knight, and trains herself in jousting and other military skills. But her father is persuaded by his wife (the second of the 'wise counsellors') to give Hrolf permission to attempt the hand of Thornbjorg, and after getting the worst of it for some time, Hrolf wins in the end by courage, skill, and sheer persistence. 'What a shrewd and patient man you are!' exclaims the conquered and admiring Thornbjorg, who thereupon pays proper courtesy to her father, hands over her weapons, retires to her boudoir, and starts work on her embroidery in preparation for marriage to Hrolf. She remains a good, faithful and feminine wife to Hrolf, only taking up arms in the latter stages of the tale to help her husband when he is in great danger; again moderation, propriety, and conformity to social and domestic order win the battle against all that is excessive and unrestrained.

When we come to the third marriage-quest, again we find a girl who refuses suitors, but this time her father is on her side and she is distinctly a daddy's girl, not at all like the amazonic Thornbjorg, and something of a spoiled brat:

The king was very fond of his daughter, and even though kings
themselves asked to marry her, they were chased off by the
scoffing and jeering of the berserks, and were very glad to get
away from these insults. This made the princess so choosy she
wouldn't say yes to anyone who wanted her, so they all got tired
of her answers, and kept out of her way.

The casualness here suggests that the reader is not intended to
take this girl too seriously. But she has the nerve to refuse
Hrolf's brother, the hot tempered Ketil, involving Hrolf too in
the marriage quest in aid of his blood-brother, and so a new
series of battles begins. The 'wise counsellor' this time is a man,
Thorir Iron-Shield, chief general to the girl Alof's father, King
Halfdan, and foster-father to Alof. In his refusal to indulge her,
he shows himself to be a better father than her natural one, who
in turn shows his own foolish wilfulness in ignoring the advice
of the moderate, thoughtful, and plainly spoken Thorir. When
Halfdan gets himself into difficulties, Alof goes to her foster-
father to try to persuade him to help Halfdan out, which
in view of Halfdan's behaviour he has previously refused to
do. Here, in contrast with the 'immoderate' masculinity of
Thornbjorg in the previous quest episode, Alof is shown to be
improper in her use of her femininity. At least Thornbjorg
asserts herself heroically, and, *as a man*, behaves with all the
virtues of the viking ideal. So, even after she has finally accepted
a submissive role as wife, she retains her distinctive character,
she can put on her armour again to help her husband in time
of need, and her husband recognises the continuing duality of

15

her nature, admirably kept in proper balance once she has acknowledged the feminine element (see p. 67). Compare this with the more insinuating feminine skills of Alof: she tries calling her foster-father a coward, but when this doesn't work she attempts a softer approach:

> She hesitated whether or not to go back once more to her foster-father to plead with him, but at last she went up to him boldly, put her arms round his neck and said, 'Dear foster-father, I beg you, help my father so that I won't be married against my will. You've promised to grant me one request if I ask you, and now I want you to go into battle and give my father all the support you can. I know you'll fight well.'
>
> Thorir Iron-Shield knocked the girl flat on the ground and seemed so angry she didn't dare speak to him. Then as he sprang to his feet she heard him fetch a deep groan. He seized his weapons, put on his armour quickly with a practised hand, and ran to the battlefield. . . .

She is seen as essentially wilful, like Thornbjorg, but in a different way. Thornbjorg can never become a mere piece of property, concerned as she is, even after her conquest, with aiding and advising, not merely using her husband or acting a purely passive role. But Alof is too feminine for the masculine world of the tale, she is barely mentioned after this episode, and her ultimate place in the scheme of things is made fairly clear when we are told that Hrolf's army 'sailed away from Russia with the bride they'd won, and all the other valuable things'.

The fourth and final marriage-quest is undertaken on behalf of Hrolf's blood-brother Asmund, to ask for the daughter of King Hrolf of Ireland. The fathers of the brides, it will be noticed, have been represented as increasingly immoderate in the way they conduct marriage dealings, and Hrolf of Ireland is positively the worst. He does not even attempt, as Halfdan did, to kill Hrolf Gautreksson in battle, but captures him and plans to starve him to death in a pit floored with corpses: yet another contrast between the moderate and immoderate is made by setting Hrolf of Ireland's conduct in this episode against the courtesy and tact of Ælla of England, at whose court Hrolf Gautreksson stays on his way to Ireland. Again, moderation begets moderation, and when Hrolf, in return for Ælla's courtesy, asks for clemency to be shown his enemies at court, his conduct enhances his honour. But the Irish court, by contrast, is a place of violence and cruelty: the exception is Ingibjorg, the king's daughter (her name is the same, incidentally, as that of the other moderating woman who chose Gautrek in the first marriage-quest and became Hrolf's mother). Significantly, and unromantically, it is not Asmund, her suitor, who attracts her sympathy with his love-quest, so much as Hrolf Gautreksson with his honourable reputation:

The daughter of the King of Ireland had been watching the battle all day and admiring the brave fight King Hrolf Gautreksson had been putting up, along with his men. She was far from happy that the life of such an outstanding king should have to be cut short like that.

So she sends one of her girls over to the pit where Hrolf Gautreksson and Asmund are trapped – but it is Hrolf Gautreksson to whom she addresses the message:

> When the battle was over, the princess called the girl to her and said, 'Go over to the pit where King Hrolf Gautreksson and his men are held captive, and ask him what he would like me to do for him most, if I could.'

In due course, Hrolf Gautreksson is rescued, gives Hrolf of Ireland his life, in the chivalric tradition, upon his daughter's request and as a courtesy to her, and the saga ends in a welter of arranged marriages.

The blood-brotherhood theme, too, points a contrast between moderation and excess, principally by continually highlighting Hrolf Gautreksson's coolness and courtesy against the background of his brother Ketil's foolhardiness. Again and again we see how Ketil recommends, and involves himself (and others, including Hrolf) in immediate, unconsidered action and its consequences, while Hrolf chooses to wait, to consider, and only to act when the best course is clear – though when the moment for action comes, no one ever outdoes Hrolf in energy and decisiveness. The characteristic contrast can be seen in the following episode, in which Ketil comes off worse in an encounter with Thornbjorg, the Swedish 'king' (bear in mind that she insists on being addressed as a man):

> King Hrolf had a word with his brother Ketil. 'I want you to start moving against this Swedish king and take him captive

if you can. But you mustn't use weapons on him for it's a cowardly thing to wound a woman with weapons.'

Ketil promised to do his best. Then the Swedes were routed. Ketil got so close he was able to bang the Swedish king on the backside with the flat of his sword. 'Lady,' he said, 'here's how we cure your itching crutch. That's what I call a dirty stroke!'

The king said, 'This stroke won't bring you any honour,' and then she hit Ketil with an axe under the ear so hard he was knocked head over heels. 'This is how we usually beat our dogs when they bark too loud,' she said.

Ketil jumped to his feet looking for revenge, but just then King Hrolf came up and laid hands on King Thorberg. 'Lay down your weapons, sir,' said Hrolf, 'you're in my hands now. I'll spare the lives of all your men if you promise to do as your father says.'

The King of the Swedes said, 'I take it, King Hrolf, that you think you've got us all in your power, but it won't bring you any credit to force us into anything against our will.'

King Hrolf said, 'Look, sir, now we've met like this, I can only think of your honour. I'm going to ask your father to settle the whole issue, and if he's the one to judge between us, everybody will agree about the safety of your dignity and honour.'

In fact, so central is this theme of Hrolf's courtesy and self-control against Ketil's (often quite amiable) discourtesy and foolhardiness that the first two paragraphs of the final chapter are largely given over to a comparison between the two men in these terms: thus Ketil 'gained more of a reputation for his courage, ambition, arrogance and enthusiasm, than for his wisdom and wit', whereas Hrolf 'became the strongest of rulers, and plenty of people looked to him for friendship, expecting to derive peace and freedom from his strength, instead of the war and oppression that many others had to suffer from.'

HROLF GAUTREKSSON was not created in literary isolation. It has a great deal in common with a number of other stories written in Iceland during the first part of the fourteenth century, when realistic fiction in the classical saga tradition was coming to an end. This was still a lively period of literary activity, but after *Grettir's Saga* (*c.*1320–30) no major story on native Icelandic themes was attempted. Gradually the saga authors were ceasing to explore the well-mapped history of early Iceland and instead were turning their attention to antiquity, to the remote and nebulous Scandinavian past with its vikings, valkyries, trolls, and demons. These late authors resuscitated warriors from the viking period and stranger figures from even shadowier times, clothing them in the dress of figures from another source, as we have said, the knightly world of the Age of Chivalry. The vikings were transformed into the urbanised occupants of castles and fortified towns, mixing their northern heroic violence with southern idealisation and courtesy. Out of the synthesis of these apparently irreconcilable cultures, the saga writers of late medieval Iceland produced their own curious hybrid art.

The writers of this period appear to have known each others' tales, and there is a certain degree of cross-fertilisation. Mention might be made, for instance, of affinities between *Hrolf Gautreksson* and the saga of his father, Gautrek, to which we have referred earlier. At one point in *Gautrek's Saga* there is even a hint that *Hrolf Gautreksson* might be by the same author, when we are told:

> After that King Eirik was the sole ruler of Sweden for a long time, as will be told elsewhere in *Hrolf Gautreksson's Saga*.[5]

But the style and, apart from the final episode, the content of *Gautrek's Saga* are rather different from *Hrolf Gautreksson*, though it may be significant that the passages indicating connexions between the two sagas all occur within a page or so, at the point where the narrative shifts from the heroic episode of Starkad and Vikar, with its interest in a tragic Grettir-like hero and his dealings with the old gods of the north, to the Romance-style marriage-quest of Ref Rennison. In these transitional passages, reference is made to Gautrek's mourning of his wife on her grave mound,[6] which is taken up by the author of *Hrolf Gautreksson* as the starting point of the first of his four episodes of the marriage quest. The story of Ref Rennison is much more like *Hrolf Gautreksson* than any other part of *Gautrek's Saga*, concerned as it is with Ref's marriage-quest under the guidance of Earl Neri, a 'wise counsellor' figure akin to those of *Hrolf Gautreksson*. And yet another link is the

---

5. *Gautrek's Saga*, tr. Pálsson & Edwards, p. 42.
6. *Op. cit.*, p. 43.

reference, in the paragraph immediately before the one about Gautrek's mourning his wife, to the gift of horses offered to Hrosskel:

King Gautrek had a number of important men with him. One of his friends was a great viking called Hrosskel. On one occasion King Gautrek invited him to a feast, and when it was over, he gave Hrosskel some excellent parting gifts: a grey stallion and four mares, silk-pale and splendid. Hrosskel thanked the king for the presents and they parted the best of friends.[7]

But in *Hrolf Gautreksson* this friendly and courteous gesture of Gautrek's is given a grotesque turn, and made the basis of an accusation of sexual abnormality in Hrolf's gibing tale against Hrosskel and the vikings. In *Gautrek's Saga* there is not the least hint of this, and the superficiality of these links suggests that the later tale is not so much a continuation of *Gautrek's Saga*, as a sequel to it.

Hrolf Gautreksson ends on a none-too-serious note of self-questioning on the part of the story-teller of the historicity of the tale. 'People say this is a true story,' he writes, tongue-in-cheek, for it is clear by the end of the paragraph that the story-teller sees his tale very much more as entertainment than as history. He goes on to put forward a medieval theory of evolution, explaining the disappearance of giants as a con-

---

7. *Op. cit.*, p. 42.

sequence of racial mixing and the earlier existence of giants in terms of natural selection:

> It shouldn't surprise anyone that people used to be bigger and stronger than they are now, because it looks as if their claim to be descended from giants could be true, and not so far back either. But now people are levelling out as the races get mixed. It's likely that a lot of small men would have been killed by the strokes of the big ones, since weapons in those days were so heavy that the weaker sort could hardly have been able to lift them off the ground. It's obvious that small men wouldn't be very likely to survive being hit with such strong blows and sharp edges.

Thus, finally, we can see the difference between those tales, the Sagas of Icelanders and the Kings' Sagas, whose authors were sharply aware of their historical content, and the Legendary Sagas such as *Hrolf Gautreksson* in which the historical element is blurred, the remoteness of the tale being marked here by the differences between the lives of the figures in the narrative on one hand, and those of the author and his public on the other. This leads us to the author's last observation made in the epilogue to the tale, an aesthetic one. 'I don't think it right,' he says, 'to find fault with a story unless you can improve it.' So he invites us to respect the integrity of his tale not as history, but as art and entertainment, and we might make the same plea now as its anonymous author made some six centuries ago: 'whether it's true or not, let those enjoy the story who can, while those who can't had better look for some other amusement.'

List of characters

GAUTREK	*King of Gotaland*
INGIBJORG	*his second Queen*
HROLF & KETIL	*their sons*
HRING, *King of Denmark*	Hrolf's *foster-father*
INGJALD, *his son*	Hrolf's *blood-brother*
EIRIK	*King of Sweden*
INGIGERD	*his Queen*
THORNBJORG ('King Thorberg')	*their daughter*
OLAF	*King of Scotland*
ASMUND	*his son,* Hrolf's *blood-brother*
MARGARET	*King Olaf's daughter*
HALFDAN	*King of Russia*
ALOF	*his daughter*
THORIR IRON-SHIELD	*King Halfdan's chief counsellor*
HROLF	*King of Ireland*
INGIBJORG	*his daughter*
SIGRID	*her handmaid*
ÆLLA	*King of England*
GRIM	*farmer's son, in England*
THORD	*farmer, in England*
GYDA	Thord's *sister*

GRIMAR GRIMOLFSSON, GRIMNIR GRIMOLFSSON, HAREK, HROSSKEL, HORSE-HEAD, & HORSE-THIEF
berserks and vikings

24

HROLF GAUTREKSSON

CHAPTER I

The suitors

OUR STORY BEGINS when King Gautrek, son of King Gauti, was ruler of Gotaland. In many ways he was a fine king, very popular, and so open-handed that whenever people talk about the ancient kings, his name is still a by-word. He had an only daughter, and on the advice of Earl Neri he married her off to Gift-Ref Rennisson.

By this time King Gautrek's wife was dead, and he himself was getting on in years, though he was still a vigorous man. He'd felt the loss of his wife so deeply that he used to spend most of the time sitting on her gravemound, and he was so bitter about her death he was letting the country go to pieces. So his friends begged him to marry again, and told him they wanted no-one but his descendants to rule over them. They also said they felt sure it would bring honour and lasting happiness to everyone concerned, once he got himself a good wife. King Gautrek took the suggestion in good part, and said they were showing him the same goodwill now that they'd always shown by giving him their advice and their loyal support. A little later, King Gautrek got ready for a journey and set off with eighty men, a splendid looking war-band, finely dressed and well fitted out with weapons. He wanted only the best for this journey, as was proper to his dignity.

Over in Norway, there was a powerful chieftain called Thorir. His residence was in Sogn, where he was held in high respect, being a man of distinction and noble ancestry. He was married, with an only daughter called Ingibjorg, an intelligent good-looking girl. People thought her a great match. A number of important men had asked to marry her, but she didn't think any of them good enough for her, and had turned them all down.

So it came about that King Gautrek arrived there with his retinue, and was given a great reception. Thorir went to meet him and invited him to stay there with his companions for as long as he liked. King Gautrek was treated to a magnificent feast, with all that was best in entertainment and hospitality. A certain prince from far away called Olaf was also visiting there with a hundred companions, to ask for Ingibjorg's hand, and she'd given him a favourable answer. This Olaf was a young man of good prospects. Gautrek heard about it but paid no attention, and after he'd been there some time he took Thorir aside to have a word with him in private.

'I'd like to tell you the reason for my visit,' said King Gautrek. 'I've been told you've a clever good-looking daughter called Ingibjorg. I've made up my mind to ask for her as my wife and by way of this family alliance I'll pledge my friendship to you.'

Thorir said, 'I've heard reliable reports that you're a chieftain of great importance, and that's why I'd like to give you a favourable answer. Most likely you'd make my daughter a good husband. But the fact of the matter is, a young prince called

Olaf with good prospects has made her an offer of marriage, and we've already had several sessions with him about it. It's a dilemma I can get out of if I tell Ingibjorg to choose her own husband, which is just what she's already asked me to do.'

Both suitors were very satisfied with this arrangement, and a little later the three men went with their friends over to Ingibjorg's boudoir. When she saw her father with these two distinguished visitors, she welcomed them all warmly and invited them to take a seat.

Thorir opened the discussion. 'This is how it is, daughter, these two kings you see here have come with me just to meet you, for one and the same reason: they want to propose marriage. But since the old saying always holds good, "You can't get two sons-in-law for one daughter," what I want now is for you to make your own choice, whichever of the two you'd prefer for a husband. I want you to give them straight answers and I hope what you decide will be to your own credit, and that we'll all benefit from it.'

Ingibjorg answered, 'As I see it, this is far too delicate a problem for me to handle sensibly, or for any other woman with as little experience as I have; and it's far from certain that I'd make the best choice for myself. I think it's quite clear that both kings are very great men and more than good enough for me, whichever of them ultimately looks after me. But bearing in mind certain precedents, this is the conclusion I've come to: these two kings might be compared with two apple trees standing in the same orchard. One is young and promises to yield a fine crop of big, sweet-tasting apples before reaching the

full ripeness of his life; that's the tree that stands for King Olaf.
Besides this, there's another apple tree with lots of branches,
heavy with all kinds of apples. That tree stands for King
Gautrek's authority and power, for his long reign has been
marked by his generosity and distinction, and now his kingdom
is in full flower. We all know how brave and open-handed he is,
and if his reign were to be cut short by natural causes, perhaps
he could still have begotten sturdy sons to make up for the loss.
So although Olaf is the younger man and likely to make a
splendid king, to pay for a promise is always a risky bargain.
I'm not going to elaborate on this any further just now, but the
one I choose is King Gautrek, to live with and to enjoy. Even if
I knew for certain that he'd only live for a few years and that
Olaf was fated to grow as old as a stone bridge, I've a feeling he
could never be as great a king as Gautrek, and certainly not if
Olaf hasn't all that long to live.'

King Gautrek was delighted to hear what the girl had to say;
he jumped to his feet like a young man, took hold of her hand,
and betrothed himself to her there and then, right in front of
King Olaf.

This put Olaf into a great rage, and he swore he'd take
revenge on King Gautrek and his men. Gautrek said that a man
nothing could touch wasn't likely to come to grief, and with that
they parted, King Olaf setting off with his followers in an ugly
mood.

CHAPTER 2

The Sons

K ING GAUTREK STAYED ON for as long as he felt like it and then got ready to go back home with Ingibjorg, his bride to be, for he wanted to celebrate their wedding in Gotaland. Thorir gave his daughter a generous dowry, with plenty of gold and silver, and King Gautrek set out with his men on his journey back home. One day when they were travelling past a certain forest, King Olaf and his troops intercepted them, and fierce fighting broke out.

When they'd been fighting for some time, King Olaf said, 'Would you like me to give you a chance to save your life, King Gautrek? Just let me have the girl and all the wealth she's got as her dowry, and then you can go in peace wherever you want. It's not decent, an old man like you lechering over such a lovely young girl. It's your one chance to get out of this alive.'

King Gautrek listened to what he said, and replied, 'Even though my men are fewer than yours, you'll find out before the day's over that there's one old man here who's not afraid of you.'

King Gautrek was so keen that he scythed his way time and again right through Olaf's army, and he didn't stop till Olaf and all his men were dead. Gautrek won the victory with hardly any loss of life, then carried on with his journey and kept going until he arrived back home to Gotaland, with his fame very much enhanced.

Shortly after his return he began preparing a lavish feast

and invited all the important people in the land. He drank the wedding toast to Ingibjorg in the strongest beer there was, and when the feast was over he gave splendid gifts to all the great people who had attended it. All this added a great deal to his fame.

King Gautrek and his wife came to love one another dearly. They lived quietly at home for a time, and not too long afterwards Gautrek gave his wife a boy. The child was brought to his father, who had him sprinkled with water and gave him a name. He was called Ketil, and grew up at court there.

Three years later Ingibjorg gave birth to another boy; he was big and handsome, and was called Hrolf. Both boys were given an education fit for princes, but they turned out to be very unlike one another. Ketil was extremely small, boisterous, ambitious, impulsive, and full of drive and grit. He was so tiny he was nicknamed Ketil Mite. Hrolf was unusually tall and strong, and very handsome. He was a man of few words, always honoured his promises, and wasn't over-ambitious. Whenever something was done or said against him, he used to pretend he hadn't noticed, but later, when it was least expected, he was ruthless in taking his revenge. When people tried to sway his opinion about something that concerned him, he used to pay no attention to begin with, but afterwards, perhaps years later, apparently having thought things out fully, he'd raise it again no matter whether it was good or bad for him. Once he'd made up his mind, he had to have his way. He was well-liked by everyone, and some people were very fond of him. And so time passed till Ketil was ten years old, and Hrolf seven.

CHAPTER 3
The foster-father

AT THAT TIME there was a powerful and popular king ruling in Denmark called Hring. He was married and his queen was good-looking and clever. They had an only son called Ingjald, a promising youngster. King Gautrek and Hring were close friends, and they used to exchange gifts, invite each other to feasts, and bestow royal honours on one another as long as this friendship lasted. They'd fought side by side in their younger days, and as long as they saw plenty of one another they stayed friends. But the time came when disagreement began to creep into their relationship, evil tongues spreading slander between them. This went so far, they started preparing for war against one another.

One day Hring of Denmark had a talk with his wife. 'You know how I've been warned that King Gautrek plans to mount an attack on our land, though I've never been able to find out what he's got against us. Now, it seems a good idea to get the first blow in; as the saying goes, "The aggressor lands on top." But I'm not sure people have been altogether fair, accusing him of the intrigues I've been told about.'

The Queen said, 'You're talking nonsense, considering what good friends you've been, to let the slander of the wicked set you against King Gautrek. This isn't kingly, wanting to destroy your own blood-brother, and if it really comes to the worst, better for you to let him play you false than do him any harm yourself and lose his friendship. Do as I ask you, my lord, rid your heart of all these treacherous thoughts before they pull down and trample on all the good things you two have given each other. Hold on fast to the bonds of goodwill between you and Gautrek, my lord, hold to them nobly and honestly. Love him, keep peace with him, don't lose the friendship of a good man like that just for the sake of wicked people's gossip. He's taken a wife with so much good sense and goodwill, she'll bring you together again and heal the breach. King Gautrek has fine sons too, who'd soon take revenge if their father were offended in any way. You take my advice, my lord, go with all your wisest counsellors in a single ship to King Gautrek, and offer fosterage to his son Hrolf. If they accept the offer, he'll strengthen your kingdom and your power for the rest of your days, and bring honour to us all.'

That was the end of the Queen's speech. The King thought she'd spoken wisely and well and said he'd no intention of ignoring her advice. He prepared for the voyage as the Queen had suggested, put out to sea as soon as he was ready and arrived in Gotaland safe and sound.

When King Gautrek was told about Hring's arrival, he asked Queen Ingibjorg to come and have a word with him. 'I've been told,' he said, 'that Hring of Denmark's landed in our kingdom with a single ship. You know already how hostile he's said to be towards us, and now I'm going to pay him back in full before we part. He's fallen right into my hands and this time I can get my own way without risking a single life.'

The Queen heard him out, then she said, 'This harangue of

yours makes no sense. Here's Hring come to visit you, apparently hoping you'll show him the same honour and goodwill you used to treat each other with, and you want to harm the man. Look at it this way. Hring would never have come here with such a small following if he didn't trust you just as much as he used to, so those must have been lies about his being against you. This is what I suggest: send a messenger to meet him and invite him with all his retinue to a magnificent feast here. Be cheerful and pleasant to him, and when he comes into the hall with his men, pay close attention and see if he's guilty of anything he's been charged with. If you find there's any disagreement between you, settle it with the advice of all the best men, and afterwards stick to your blood-brotherhood without any more troubles as long as you live.'

The King took note of the Queen's advice and prepared a lavish feast, inviting not only Hring of Denmark with all his retinue, but a good many other wise and important people as well whom he also wanted to consult. The Kings sat down in the hall, started enjoying themselves, and tried to sort out who'd been responsible for the breach in their friendship. Once they started questioning one another they soon found out who'd been undermining their goodwill. As soon as they realised that the only disagreement between them was caused by the slander and malicious gossip of wicked people, they renewed their old friendship. The first step was that Hring offered fosterage to Hrolf Gautreksson, and King Gautrek accepted this gladly. Then Hring got ready for his voyage back home, and Hrolf went with him. Hring set out to sea with splendid gifts, and both kings were delighted with this outcome. They parted the best of friends and remained on affectionate terms for the rest of their lives.

Hrolf went to Denmark with Hring, who gave him an excellent upbringing and provided him with the best tutor in the whole of Scandinavia. This master taught him all the skills that brave and strong men at the time could wish for. Hrolf and Ingjald became very close friends, and entered into blood-brotherhood. So these two boys grew up there in Denmark, and Hrolf turned out to be a remarkable man, stronger and bigger than anyone else. But Ketil grew up with his father in Gotaland, the smallest of men and very agile. King Gautrek didn't take to Ketil, because he didn't like his boisterous and aggressive nature.

CHAPTER 4

The Amazon

THERE WAS A KING ruling over Sweden called Eirik; he was married to a clever and charming queen, and they had an only daughter called Thornbjorg. She was unusually good-looking and intelligent, and people thought there wasn't a girl to compare with her. She was brought up at home by her father and mother, and it's said she was better at all the feminine arts than any other woman. She used to tilt on horseback too, and learnt to fence with sword and shield, mastering these arts as

perfectly as any knight trained in the courtly skill of plying his
weapons.

King Eirik wasn't at all happy to see her taking part in such
masculine sports, and told her to stay in her boudoir like other
princesses. This is how she answered him. 'Since you've been
given only one life to govern this kingdom and I'm your only
child and heir,' she said, 'it seems very likely that I'll have to
defend it against a few kings or princes, once you're gone. It's
also hardly likely I'll be very keen to marry any-one against my
will, if it ever comes to that, and that's why I want to get to
know something of the skills of knighthood. It seems to me that
would give me a better chance of holding on to this kingdom,
with the help of strong and reliable followers. So I want you,
father, to put me in charge of some part of your kingdom while
you're still alive, so that I can try my hand at government and
commanding the men entrusted to me. There's one more point:
if any-one asks to marry me and I don't want him, there'll be a
better chance of your kingdom being left in peace if you leave
the answers to me.'

The King thought over what the girl had said and realised
what a shrewd but wilful woman she was. It seemed to him
quite possible that his kingdom might suffer through her pride
and arrogance, but he decided to give her control over a third of
the realm. He fortified her residence at Ullarakur, too, and gave
her tough and sturdy men as followers, obedient men, willing to
do whatever she wanted.

When she'd got all this out of her father, she moved over to
Ullarakur. Next she held a big assembly and had herself elected

as king over one third of Sweden, just as King Eirik had agreed. At the same time she changed her name to 'Thorberg', and anyone so bold as to call her a maiden or woman was in serious trouble. Then 'King Thorberg' started dubbing knights and appointing courtiers, and gave them pay the same as King Eirik of Uppsala, and that's how things stood in Sweden for some years.

CHAPTER 5

Gautrek dies

NOW WE PICK UP the story of King Gautrek of Gotaland. He fell ill and sent for his queen and other important people. 'It's like this,' he said to them, 'I've a sickness, and since I'm getting on in years it'll probably be my last. I'd like to thank everyone from my heart for their support and loyalty. As you know, I've two sons who're my heirs, one living with us here, and the other with Hring in Denmark. It's the law of this land that the older son must succeed to the throne and kingdom after his father, and I don't wish to break the law against my son Ketil, or against you, my subjects, by insisting on my own way, but I beg of you all, let the one I think best for the throne be my successor.'

They said they'd gladly follow his advice, as it had always been good enough for them, and added that they certainly weren't going to overrule his last wishes, considering they'd always done as he told them in the past, and always to their advantage.

Then the King said he wanted Hrolf to succeed to the throne, as he expected him to become an outstanding man and a fine leader. The King asked Ketil not to take this badly, and Ketil said he wasn't all that keen to govern and was quite content for Hrolf to take over the kingdom. Then the men thanked the King for all the peace and prosperity they'd enjoyed for so long under his firm rule and royal guidance.

So the King made all the arrangements he thought important, and after that everyone went back home, apart from those appointed to sit beside him. It wasn't long before this illness brought the King's death. The Queen and everyone else in the kingdom took his death very much to heart; all his subjects mourned him deeply, for his generosity and thoughtfulness had made him more loved than any other King. Then, according to the old custom, King Gautrek was buried in a grave-mound.

Shortly afterwards the Queen got herself ready for a journey and travelled with a magnificent retinue all the way to Hring in Denmark. When she met the King she told him of her loss and the grief she'd suffered at the death of King Gautrek, and about all the arrangements Gautrek had made before he died. Hring was saddened by the news and felt the death of his sworn-brother deeply. He invited Ingibjorg to stay there as long as she pleased.

The Queen said, 'We've not made this journey just to settle down in your kingdom, and if you want to honour us, sir, I'd like to ask you to come over to Gotaland with your foster-son

Hrolf, so that with your guidance he can get himself well-established, as King Gautrek ordered. I'd also like you to attend the funeral feast we're giving in honour of King Gautrek according to the old customs.'

The King promised to do as she asked; and not long after he set out on a journey with a fine retinue. He didn't stop till he'd reached Gotaland along with Queen Ingibjorg and her son Hrolf. A magnificent feast awaited them there, attended by many of the leading people in the kingdom. After they'd celebrated King Gautrek's funeral feast, a great assembly was held, and there, with Hring's guidance and the approval of all the people of Gotaland, Hrolf was made King.

When all this had been done, Hring went back to Denmark, loaded with magnificent gifts. Hrolf took charge of the kingdom and started making new laws and statutes as he saw fit. He soon grew popular with all his people, for he was an able and generous ruler, just as his father had been. Hrolf was twelve years old when he took on the authority of government and kingship over the land.

His brother Ketil used to stay with him, but his blood-brother Ingjald would go on viking expeditions in the summer and spend the winter with the King in Gotaland. So time passed till Hrolf was fifteen years old.

CHAPTER 6

To seek a wife

THE STORY GOES that one day when the brothers were talking together, Hrolf asked Ketil what he thought of his future as a ruler and leader of men. Ketil said he was quite satisfied with Hrolf in most respects.

'Since you've qualified your praises,' said Hrolf, 'tell me where I fall short in anything I'm responsible for.'

'I can easily find one flaw in your splendour,' said Ketil. 'You're not married yet, and you'd be thought much more of if you'd get yourself a suitable wife.'

'Whereabouts should we look?' asked the King.

'It would do a lot for your prestige,' said Ketil, 'if you'd propose to a princess who has both judgment and foresight, and it seems obvious to me that wherever you try, your proposal's not going to be turned down.'

'I'm not concerned about that just yet,' said the King. 'This is a small kingdom and nobody's going to find it very attractive to join me on the throne. Where did you think we might look around, kinsman?'

'I've been told King Eirik of Sweden has a clever, good-looking daughter called Thornbjorg,' said Ketil. 'I've heard there's no better match throughout the whole of Scandinavia, she's an ornament of womanhood, and in some things she's the equal of the most valiant knights, at jousting and fencing with sword and shield. That's something she's got over all the other women I've ever heard of. Eirik her father's an outstanding king not only for his great authority, but for plenty of other things that make a king truly magnificent.'

King Hrolf answered, 'I'm not bold enough for that sort of venture. What you say shows more ardour than foresight, and not for the first time either. It's ridiculous when a man fools himself into aiming far beyond his powers. It seems likely to me that if I go and ask to marry the daughter of King Eirik of Sweden as you want me to, I'll be turned down, and then probably have to take a few nasty insults into the bargain. I'd have to stand for it all, too, as I've no way of taking my revenge on a king as powerful as him, and I'm not the man to put up with that.'

Ketil said it would never come to that. 'We've plenty of troops from Denmark and Gotaland to fight King Eirik if he won't have you as a son-in-law.'

'There's no need to go on about it,' said Hrolf. 'I know exactly how it'll turn out if we try it.'

It was typical of Hrolf's temper that he paid no more attention to this. He ignored it just like so many other suggestions made to him, and no-one knew what was going on in his mind, but he would bring a matter up later when every-one else had forgotten all about it. So time passed, and the blood-brothers based themselves alternately in Denmark and Gotaland, and spent the summers on viking expeditions. They were the toughest of fighting-men and took a great deal of loot, for nothing could stop them. Their exploits made them famous far and wide, and their names became a by-word.

King Hrolf is described as an exceptionally big strong man, and so heavy that he couldn't ride the same horse for a whole day because it would suffocate or collapse under him, so his men had to keep exchanging horses with him. Hrolf was a handsome, courteous man, faultlessly built, with a fine head of hair, a broad, strong-featured face, eyes like no other man's, bright and piercing, a slender waist and broad shoulders, well-proportioned and superbly-bred, an outstanding fighter and better at all sports than any of his contemporaries in Scandinavia. Everybody loved him. King Hrolf was a shrewd man of unusual foresight, a knowledgeable and sharp-witted man, and his kingliness soon gained him a reputation abroad and at home.

One spring Ketil asked King Hrolf what he planned to do in the summer.

'Wouldn't it be a good idea,' Hrolf answered, 'to go to Sweden and see about a marriage alliance with King Eirik as you suggested once?'

'You're a strange one,' said Ketil, 'First you turn a completely deaf ear to what you've been told and don't even bother to think about it, even though it's in your own interest. Then years later you bring it up again and talk about it as if it's just been mentioned. I've still not changed my mind and I think it's a matter that can't wait.'

'Have you heard anything about this girl?' asked the King.

'Nothing at all, apart from what I've told you already,' said Ketil.

'I've been told she's good-looking and intelligent,' said the King, 'and I've also been told she's so proud and arrogant she won't let any-one address her as a woman. She's been made king over a third of Sweden and keeps a royal court at Ullarakur just like any other king. They tell me several kings have proposed to her already; some of them she's had killed, and others maimed one way or another, some blinded, some castrated, some have had their arms or legs cut off, and she's ridiculed and insulted everybody. That's how she wants to put them off trying their luck with her. I can see well enough, this business is bound to end one of two ways: if we manage to get the woman, we'll boost our reputations a good deal by this trip; on the other hand we run the risk of suffering such shame and humiliation, we'd be a laughing-stock for the rest of our lives.'

Ketil said, 'You're a puny-hearted one, for all your size and strength. No wonder people keep making fun of you, if you don't even have the nerve to put a little question to a woman. What I think is this, the more arrogance she shows, the harder her pride's going to fall when the time comes, and that will be the end of that.'

'Since you've questioned whether I've the nerve for the business,' said King Hrolf, 'I'm sending you over to Denmark for my blood-brother Ingjald. I want him to join me on this trip.'

After that they dropped the subject, and Ketil got ready to sail to Denmark. Ingjald wasted no time and hurried to meet King Hrolf, who welcomed him warmly and told him what he had in mind. Ingjald liked the idea and said that with the King's good luck they could be sure things would turn out well, even if they were to take some time. King Hrolf told his brother Ketil to stay behind and look after the kingdom.

'Have it your own way, my lord, though I'm a bit surprised you don't think I'm man enough to go with you,' said Ketil.

'You mustn't think that, brother,' answered the King, 'you'll join me on other missions where real courage is needed. But this time we're going to try to get what we want with tact and moderation, if we can.'

So Ketil was forced to stay behind, but he warned them they would have to pay dearly for it. King Hrolf set off with sixty riders, all handpicked men, nobly born and fitted out with the best of clothes and weapons. On their way they rode and kept going till they came to Uppsala.

CHAPTER 7

A dream

NOW WE COME BACK to King Eirik. He was married to a clever and handsome wife called Ingigerd, who was particularly interested in dreams. One night the Queen woke up in bed and started talking to the King. 'I must have been very restless in my sleep,' she said.

'Yes, you were,' said the King. 'What were you dreaming about, then?'

She said, 'I seemed to be standing outside taking a look around me, and then suddenly I thought I could see the whole of Sweden and even far beyond. When I looked towards

43

Gotaland, it was all so clear that I could see a huge pack of wolves there, and they seemed to be making for Sweden. Leading the wolves was a lion, a really big one, and behind it came a polar bear, very savage-looking it was. Both creatures seemed to have smooth unruffled pelts and looked very quiet and peaceable, but what struck me as really strange was that they were travelling at such a fantastic speed. I could see clearly, there were at least sixty of them. I was certain they were making for Uppsala. It seemed I was calling out to you to tell you about it when I woke up.'

'What's the meaning of this, do you think, my lady?' asked the King.

'The wolves I seemed to see must have stood in my dream for men,' she said. 'The lion ahead of them must have been their king leading them, and the polar bear running beside him must have been a warrior or prince accompanying the king, since the bear's a strong animal and signifies a firm supporter. So I think it very likely that some great king will soon be paying you a visit. The lion was much bigger and stronger than any other I've ever heard of.'

The King said, 'Where do you think this king's coming from? How much of a threat is this to our kingdom?'

'If I were to hazard a guess,' said the Queen, 'I'd say this king's not coming to you in enmity this time, for all these creatures looked cheerful; and if I were to make another guess, I'd say the great lion must be King Hrolf Gautreksson of Gotaland, for that's where the creatures were coming from, and I think the polar bear must be Ingjald, his blood-brother.'

'What could the warrior Hrolf be wanting from us?' asked the King.

The Queen said, 'That's a riddle we'll have to solve. But since the animals were so happy to look at, I think they must be coming in peace and friendship. I think it most likely that King Hrolf's coming on the same business as so many before him, to propose to your daughter Thornbjorg. She's the most famous woman in Scandinavia these days.'

The King said, 'I'd never have thought that King Hrolf, or any other man ruling a tiny kingdom like his, would make such a fool of himself; she's already had proposals from kings with power over tributary lands. So don't talk such nonsense, my lady.'

The Queen said, 'Don't pay any attention to me unless I've hit on the truth.'

'How should I receive King Hrolf if he comes here?' asked the King. 'And what should I say to his proposal, if that's the business he's coming on?'

'If King Hrolf comes to visit you, give him a really friendly welcome,' she said, 'and show him every consideration, because he's a remarkable man in many ways. It's not likely your daughter will get a better husband than Hrolf, if he's as good as he's said to be.'

They said nothing more about it, and several days went by.

CHAPTER 8

A proposal

K ING EIRIK WAS TOLD that King Hrolf Gautreksson had
arrived in town with sixty men. The King sent messengers
to him inviting him to a feast in the royal palace. As soon as
King Hrolf received the invitation he set out to meet King
Eirik, who gave him a respectful welcome, though without any
hint of friendship or pleasure. Hrolf was seated in the high-seat
on the lower side. It was late in the afternoon when they arrived
there, and the tables were laid for them with food and drink.
After they'd been drinking for a while, some of them got a bit
merry, but King Hrolf remained rather quiet and thoughtful.
King Eirik spoke to him and asked him the news of Gotaland
and other places he'd heard about, but King Hrolf said there was
nothing to tell about Gotaland.

'What's your business with us here in Sweden, riding with
all these men in the depths of winter?' asked King Eirik.

King Hrolf answered, 'Whatever might happen in the future,
we've always felt free to travel as we wished, by ship or on
horseback. Now that you've asked about our business I have to
say this, that we'd meant to tell you about it in our own time,
but since you've already asked about it, I don't see any reason
to put it off any longer, for the old saying's true, "The idle man
always waits till evening." My reason for coming here is that I
want to become your son-in-law and have your daughter Thornbjorg as my wife. We'd like to get a quick answer to our proposal.'

8: A PROPOSAL

'I know what a sense of humour you Gotalanders have,' said Eirik, 'you say a lot of funny things when you've been drinking' and there's no need to take them seriously. But I can make a guess as to the real reason why you've come. I've been told there's a severe famine in Gotaland, and that's not surprising, seeing that the country's small, unproductive, and heavily populated. You always feed a large army on your resources, and you're generous and openhanded as long as there's anything left. Now I suppose you must be feeling the pinch, and you've left your homeland because you couldn't stand the starvation and hardship any longer. It's really only natural that people like you should find it hard to bear conditions like these, not being able to keep up your strength; and it was very sensible of you to look for relief where it was likely to be forthcoming, rather than suffer in misery. I think well of your coming to us for help, and I can tell you right away what sort of help our realm can offer you. We're going to give you permission to travel through our kingdom for a month, and we hope you'll be thankful for this brief stay. If other kings give you the same kind of help, it's to be hoped you'll manage to get these men safely back home and so save them from starvation. But stop talking nonsense about making proposals of marriage, whether it's to my daughter or any other woman, because that can only be empty talk as long as you're so overcome by famine and poverty. Once these hard times are over, something's bound to turn up at home, so don't distress yourself over them.'

CHAPTER 9
Meeting the girl

KING HROLF LISTENED CLOSELY to the King's words and
when he'd finished, Hrolf said, 'It's not true, sir, that we're
short of food in our country or in need of other people's charity
to help us. And even if we had to cope with hardships like these,
you'd be the last man we'd come to. I think your insulting
remarks are completely uncalled for.'

People could see that King Hrolf was furious, although he'd
said very little. After that the Kings parted, and everyone went
to bed. King Hrolf and his men were shown to some houses
where they could sleep.

King Eirik went to bed, and found his queen waiting for him.
They started talking.

She asked, 'Has King Hrolf come to see you?'

'He has indeed,' said Eirik.

'What do you think of King Hrolf, then?' she asked.

'I can tell you right away,' answered King Eirik. 'From what
I've seen of him, I don't think I've ever come across a bigger,
stronger man, more handsome, more courteous or better turned
out in every way.'

'That's just what I've been told about him,' said the Queen.
'Have you talked with him at all or tested his intelligence?'

The King repeated the entire conversation between them. 'In
my opinion he's far ahead of all other men in intelligence,
ability and patience.'

The Queen said, 'It was a foolish mistake for you to get on so badly with a king as great as Hrolf. After this you can expect your land to go through long periods of trouble. No matter what you may think of his small kingdom, it seems to me he'll achieve more with his courage and kingliness than all the troops of any other king in Scandinavia, for they say he's head and shoulders above all the rest.'

'It's true,' said the King, 'he's a remarkable man, and you're certainly very impressed with him. But what should we do next?'

'I've a quick suggestion, my lord,' said the Queen. 'I want you to take it easy with King Hrolf when you meet, for I tell you truly, you'll find him a rough enemy to fight against, and he's powerful support from Denmark, since he keeps close counsel with his foster-father Hring.'

'Maybe we've made an error of judgement,' said the King. 'What could I do or say to please him?'

'This is what I suggest,' said the Queen. 'After they've taken their seats tomorrow and you've all been drinking for some time, make a few cheerful remarks to King Hrolf and ask him about his exploits. I expect he'll be a bit cool for he won't have forgotten what you said. Next, ask him about his business and pretend he's never told you about it. Then if he drops hints about your previous conversation or mentions anything about it, tell him you don't remember ever having spoken to him except in a friendly sort of way, and that if you'd said anything out of place, you wish you'd never done so. Should he raise the marriage proposal again, give him a favourable answer, but point out that he has to get her own consent, as well. Be friendly and easy-going when you discuss this with him, and then I'm sure things will go well between you. All the same I doubt whether his suit will be all that easy for him, even though you've given your consent.'

After that they slept through the night.

In the morning, when they'd settled down at the tables to drink, King Eirik was in a very jovial mood and tried hard to cheer up King Hrolf's men. Hrolf listened to this and paid close attention, but said nothing. King Eirik noticed this, and said, 'The fact of the matter is, Hrolf, that as you've come to our palace as our guest, and as it seems to me you're not enjoying yourself as much as great chieftains usually do at feasts, I'd very much like you to tell us why you're so gloomy. Then we'll try to do everything we can to make you perfectly happy and contented. In that way your Royal Highness can retain your dignity and enjoy everything we can offer to add to your honour. In return we hope to hear some entertaining stories from you about your exploits, for reports of your brave actions and battles come in daily. There's a great deal we know about this already.'

'It'll be the same in this as in everything else about me,' said King Hrolf. 'You Swedes won't be the least bit impressed.'

King Eirik said, 'We've heard so much about your good looks and achievements, we don't think it's possible to praise your appearance, your courtesy and your good manners too highly. How old are you, Hrolf, by the way?'

'I'm eighteen.'

'What a remarkable man you are!' said the King. 'Where do you plan to ride when you leave here? What's your mission?'

Hrolf was surprised that he should ask this question, and expected the King to start making fun of him again. 'We've already made our business known,' he said, 'nor are we Gotalanders likely to have forgotten the answers you gave us.'

The King said, 'I don't recall your ever having told us about any business. It wouldn't become our royal status to speak to so noble a prince as you in any but the most friendly sort of way. If we've said anything to offend you, it would only go to prove the old saying, "Ale makes another man," and now we're sober we want to take it all back as if it had never been said. Now that I'm in full control of my tongue, I'd like to give a pleasant answer to your request, and that's just how it's going to be.'

King Hrolf saw that King Eirik had changed his tune, so he made the marriage proposal afresh. He spoke well and eloquently, and when he'd delivered his speech, this is what King Eirik said. 'We wish to give you a favourable answer, for it isn't likely that a greater king than you will ask us for such a marriage alliance. You must have heard our daughter isn't staying with us any more and that we've given her a third of our land for her to rule over as king. She's a proud and powerful woman, surrounded by retainers like any other king. Plenty of kings and princes have proposed to her, but she's turned them all down with words of ridicule, and she's even had some of them maimed. I don't like her behaviour at all, she keeps committing one injustice after another, and no one's allowed to call her by anything but the name of king without getting a rough handling for it. If you're determined to win her at all costs, then, as far as we're concerned, we're willing to give our consent. In return we expect you and your men to show our people and our realm peace and friendship, even if you have to fight for what you want. We're not giving her any support against you, and we're going to stay completely out of this struggle between you.'

King Hrolf said he couldn't ask any more of the King than that, and so they sealed this agreement between them. Then they carried on with their drinking and merry-making, and King Eirik proved himself the most lavish of hosts.

Three days later King Hrolf got ready to leave, and the two Kings parted the best of friends. Hrolf didn't stop till he arrived early in the morning with his retinue at Ullarakur, where Thornbjorg had her royal seat. They were told that the 'King' was sitting at table with all his retainers. Hrolf picked out the twelve bravest men he had and told them to come with him into the hall and keep their swords drawn. 'The rest of the men are to wait outside and have the horses ready,' he said.

Then he spoke to the men who were to go with him into the hall. 'This is how we'll arrange ourselves: I'll be in the lead, along with Ingjald, then the rest one after another. If it happens that we come under any kind of attack, defend yourselves the best you can, and the one who was last in must be first out. Let's put on a bold face.'

Then they went into the palace, and once they were inside they saw it was fully equipped with seats, the men sitting at table on both sides. Nobody greeted them, and everyone fell silent as Hrolf and his men came in. King Hrolf went up to the high seat, where he saw an imposing figure, fair and handsome, wearing a magnificent royal costume. Everyone in the hall was impressed by King Hrolf's stature and good looks, but no-one uttered a word.

King Hrolf took off his helmet, bowed to the King, and stuck the sword's point into the table. 'All honour to you, my lord,' he said, 'may your kingdom prosper.'

The King heard what he had said, but she didn't reply or even give him a glance. King Hrolf realised how arrogant this king must be, and said, 'I've come to see you, sir, on the advice and with the consent of King Eirik, your father, in order to favour you and advance myself by forming a union with you for pleasure and delight, so that each of us might please the other according to the dictates of nature, without any sin or sorrow.'

The King looked at him and said, 'You must be a complete fool, coming here like this, no matter what you may call yourself back home where you belong. I think I know well enough what you mean by your pleasures and delights, you must be asking us for food and drink, and that's something we'll not deny anyone who's in need of it and asks us for it. So you can go and make your request to the steward we've appointed in charge of that sort of thing and don't bother us with your begging, I don't mean to wait in attendance on you or anyone else. Get on your way quick as soon as you've satisfied your hunger and quenched your thirst, and don't disturb us or our friends any more with your insults.'

King Hrolf said, 'It's not true that we're here to beg food

and drink, we've had plenty of that already. But since we know that you're the daughter, not the son, of the King of Sweden, we're going to state our business now in plain language. With your father's consent we're asking you to become our wife, to give strength and support to our realm, and to rear and increase our offspring, those that are born to us.'

When King Thorberg heard what Hrolf said, he got into such a mad rage he didn't know what to do. He ordered all his men in the palace to seize their weapons. 'Tie up this fool who's pouring scorn on us like this and thinks he can shame and discredit us. There's not a king or fighting man able to hold his weapon who's ever had to listen to insults like these before. We'll pay him back, we'll teach petty kings to ridicule us and poke fun at the King, our father.'

King Thorberg had a complete set of arms hanging behind him, and so had all his men, but he was the first to grab his weapons, and then one after another they did the same. Now a loud din echoed through the hall, with each man egging on his neighbour. When Hrolf saw this uproar he put on his helmet and told his men to get out of the hall. The one who'd come in last was the first to leave, and meantime all the retainers went for King Hrolf, attacking him furiously. He backed away down the hall, defending himself with the shield and hitting out with his sword. They say he killed twelve men in the hall, but once he got outside he realised there was no point in fighting on because the odds were so heavy against him, and they decided to ride away as fast as they could. There was a lot of shouting and jeering as the retainers came chasing behind them, one after

54

another. King Hrolf told his men to ride off, and that's how they parted on that occasion, because the retainers had no horses ready to race after them. Most of Hrolf's men felt very relieved at being able to get away, but there's nothing more to tell of their journey till they arrived back home in Gotaland, far from satisfied with their trip.

CHAPTER 10

Preparations

THE STORY GOES that after the chase, the Swedes went back to the palace and their King ordered the hall to be cleaned up and all the dead taken away. The news spread far and wide, and Hrolf's excursion was considered a very shameful one indeed. When King Thorberg had joined his men in the hall, he asked them if they'd recognised the man who'd insulted them.

They told him the man was called Hrolf and that he was King in Gotaland. 'It's easy to recognise him,' they said, 'he's such a big handsome man.'

The King said, 'We knew right away who he was from the stories about him, he's a very remarkable man. He must be very clever and patient, and steadfast too, so it seems. The way I see it, he's not easily roused, but he's very stubborn when he wants something, and so we can expect him to pay us Swedes another visit. We'd better look around for builders, start erecting strong and sturdy defences round the town and equip it with everything that's needed to make it impregnable against iron or fire, for one thing I do know, this king's made up his mind to get us.'

Everything was carried out exactly according to the King's orders and specifications. He had war machines installed there, both catapults and fire shot. This stronghold was so secure, everybody thought it unassailable as long as there were brave men inside to defend it. Now the King thought he could settle down in peace and was cheerful and contented, waiting for what would happen next. No one was allowed anywhere near him without his permission.

CHAPTER II

On the warpath

MEANWHILE, KING HROLF was on his way back to Gotaland, none too pleased with the outcome of his trip. His brother Ketil came to meet him and asked how he'd got on. Hrolf told him exactly what had happened between himself and the King. Ketil said, 'It's shameful, having to take that from a woman, to be chased like a mare in the herd, or a dog at the sheepfold. One thing I know, if I'd been there, this trip wouldn't have turned out so disgracefully. We'd rather be killed than be hounded like scared goats before a wolf. You aren't going to wait long for your revenge, surely? You'd better be quick and collect all the fighting men you think good enough to go with you.'

'We don't care for the mad way you rush into things,' said Hrolf, 'our trip would have turned out a lot worse if we'd let ourselves be led by your recklessness. But one thing you can be sure of, I'm planning to gather forces, though I'm not going back to Sweden this summer.'

Ketil said, 'It's a great pity the Swedes should have knocked the guts out of you, so that you're too scared to take your revenge.'

The King said he wasn't paying the least attention to any of Ketil's reproaches and rages, and that he meant to follow his own counsel. The King talked very little about it, just as he usually did, whether a thing pleased him or upset him.

So the winter passed. In the spring the King got ready to sail abroad, and when he was ready he went over summer on a viking expedition with five ships, all of them big and well manned. Both Ingjald and Ketil went with him. They made widespread raids on the British Isles, in Shetland, the Hebrides, Orkney, and Scotland. They collected a great deal of loot, and late in the summer they decided to go back home.

One night they were lying at anchor to leeward of some island, with the awnings up. After they'd settled in, King Hrolf went with some of his men for a walk across the island. On the other side of it they saw nine ships lying abreast of one another. They realised these were viking ships. The King went back to his own ships and told his brother Ketil to launch a boat and find out who was in charge of this fleet. Ketil did as he was told, rowed over to the ships, and asked who the leader was.

A tall, good-looking man was standing in the poop of one of

the ships. 'If you're asking for the leader of this fleet,' he said, 'I can tell you he's called Asmund, son of King Olaf of Scotland. Who sent you here?'

Ketil replied, 'King Hrolf Gautreksson sent me to tell you he'll be here in the morning to take your ships and money, and then cut you up for the wolves, unless you hand over everything you've got here.'

Asmund said, 'We know King Hrolf Gautreksson's famous for all the triumphs he's won during his viking career, but considering I'm a prince and have plenty of fighting men you can tell King Hrolf we're not going to give up without an effort. We'll only use five of our ships against your five, we won't try to win by unfair play.'

Ketil went back to tell King Hrolf what had happened, adding that Asmund was a handsome man, and extremely gallant.

In the morning both sides got ready for battle. Asmund ordered four of his ships to keep out of it. Then the fighting started, and long, hard fighting it was. Asmund fought with great courage, and Hrolf thought he'd never dealt with braver opponents. A good many people got killed on both sides. King Hrolf realised this was no time for half measures, so he took some men with him and boarded Asmund's own ship, and there was a deal of slaughter. Asmund kept urging his men, and he himself was putting up a great struggle. Then King Hrolf came face to face with him. Though large numbers had been killed on both sides, more were dead on Asmund's. The two leaders started exchanging blows, each of them giving everything he'd got, and Hrolf said no-one was to interfere in their fight.

Asmund got badly wounded in the combat, and when Hrolf realised that Asmund was so stout-hearted it still didn't stop him from fighting, he said, 'I'd like us to take a rest and talk a bit.'

Asmund told him to have it his way, and Hrolf said, 'I've been on viking expeditions for a good many summers, and I've never come across any-one as brave as you. Since so many of your men are dead or wounded, I'm going to offer you a choice. One is that you man your ships with unwounded crews, if you insist on keeping up the fight, and then we'll carry on with the battle. The other choice is that we agree on a truce, and then I'll offer you blood-brotherhood to cement our friendship.'

Asmund said he'd prefer the second choice, 'as long as you don't accuse me and my men of cowardice.'

Hrolf said he'd never met braver men. Then he ordered the fighting to stop, and the flag of peace was hoisted. Both armies moved up to leeward of the island, and started dressing their wounds. Two of Asmund's ships and one of Hrolf's had been completely cleared. After that they swore faith to one another, never to part unless both agreed. Then Asmund divided up the remnants of his force and manned one ship with a handpicked crew, well-equipped with weapons, but sent the rest back to Scotland. He'd lost two crews, Hrolf one. All his bravest and roughest fighters he kept on his ship, then sailed with Hrolf over to Gotaland. Next to King Hrolf, Asmund was the bravest and manliest of fighting-men, yet Hrolf still stood head and shoulders above him. They spent a peaceful winter in Gotaland with plenty of merry-making. Asmund kept reminding King Hrolf the time would come for him to visit his woman in Sweden, and kept urging him to go. The King had very little to say about that journey, and it tried his patience a good deal that his brother Ketil should keep egging him on so eagerly.

In the spring King Hrolf got ready for a voyage, taking seven ships with him, every one of them well-equipped and manned with the finest crews. Then he announced to his men that he was going to Sweden. This time he didn't tell his brother Ketil to stay behind, so all three blood-brothers joined in the expedition and with these forces they set course for Sweden.

CHAPTER 12

Second visit to Sweden

ON THE NIGHT THEY ARRIVED in Sweden, Queen Ingigerd dreamed a dream which she told to King Eirik. 'I seemed to be standing outside, and, just as before, I could see into the far distance. I looked seawards and saw that a number of ships had come in to the shore, and running from the ships came a pack of wolves, led by a lion. There were two polar bears with him, fine big creatures. All three animals were running abreast, but on the other side of the lion there was this boar running. It was a smallish sort of boar, but quite fierce-looking. I've never seen anything like it. It kept burrowing into every mound as if it wanted to overturn it, every bristle on its body sticking forward. It was just as if it meant to run and snap at everything near it.

I'm convinced this lion is King Hrolf, the same that appeared to me once before. But the lion and all the other animals were a lot fiercer looking now than last time. Once they'd run ashore, they made straight for Uppsala.'

King Eirik said, 'What can you tell me about that boar? Whose fetch could it be? It wasn't there in your other dream and then there was only one bear.'

The Queen said, 'I've been told King Hrolf has a brother called Ketil, a tiny little man, very agile, full of drive and grit and always looking for a fight. I think this boar could only be Ketil, because he wasn't with his brother Hrolf last time. The two polar bears must mean that King Hrolf has got some other great man with him, either a king or a king's son. You must keep your promise to King Hrolf, my lord. He'll be thinking about getting himself a bride. There's many a man would have avenged himself sooner for the humiliation he suffered, if it's true what we've been told about his trip to Ullarakur. If it was important for you to please him last time, it's even more so now. It would be a real blow for him if he didn't get the wife he's set out to win.'

The King said he'd do as she wished.

King Eirik was told that King Hrolf had landed, so he invited Hrolf with a hundred men to a splendid feast, and King Hrolf accepted the invitation. King Eirik went to meet him with all his retainers and welcomed him cheerfully. The guests spent several nights there enjoying good entertainment, and there was nothing wanting in King Eirik's hospitality. One day, as they were drinking together, King Eirik asked King Hrolf if he meant to fetch his bride. Hrolf said he was going to risk it, no matter what the consequences.

The King said, 'It'll turn out just the way I warned you once: for this business you're going to need both cunning and determination if you're to succeed. We've been told "King" Thorberg's made great preparations. She's had a very strong fortification built, with all sorts of devices and machinery. We don't think it'll be easy to overcome. I'm going to keep all the promises I made you and give you leave to marry her, and as her dowry you can have the kingdom we've given into her charge. When we no longer govern this country you'll take charge of the whole realm, to rule after we're dead – that's to say, if you win her.'

King Hrolf thanked King Eirik for his honourable words and said he didn't ask any more of him than that.

CHAPTER 13
Conquest

SOON AFTERWARDS they got ready to leave, and travelled without stopping until they arrived at Ullarakur. Exact reports of all their movements had gone ahead of them, and the King of the Swedes had had the stronghold firmly secured so it had become absolutely impregnable. When King Hrolf and his men arrived, there was a great deal of noise and weapon-clanging in the town. You could see preparations being made everywhere. King Hrolf told his men to make camp and prepare themselves for a long stay. He asked his brother Ketil if he'd try to win the fortress with bullying and bragging. Ketil replied he'd attack just as hard as any of his men.

They slept through the night, and in the morning King Hrolf requested an audience with the Swedish King and asked him to come out on to the fortress walls so that they could each hear what the other had to stay. The King was given the message, and came outside with all his retainers.

When King Hrolf saw the King, he said, 'Sir, I beg you, listen to what we have to say, pay attention to our words. You'll remember the last visit we paid you and the reason why we went on that journey, and how you humiliated and ridiculed us. Unless we get more satisfactory answers this time, I'll raze this town and kill every man, woman, and child inside it, or else suffer death myself.'

The Swedish King heard him out, and said, 'You'll sooner be a goat-herd in Gotaland than get control over this town or over anything else that belongs to us. Go back home with your people and be grateful for getting out of this safe and sound.'

Then the Swedish King started beating his shield and wouldn't listen to another word from King Hrolf, and all the other Swedes did the same.

When Hrolf realised there was no point in arguing with the other king, he told his men to arm themselves and attack. They did as he told them, but soon had to fall back as they were getting nowhere. Whatever they tried, there was always a counter move. They tried to set fire to the ramparts, but then water started gushing out from pipes that had been laid there. When they tried to attack with weapons or to dig under the walls, the defenders poured burning pitch and boiling water over them. They were attacked with huge boulders as well, that crushed everything in their way. There was plenty of man-power inside the fortress, and some of the attackers got killed, and a good many were hurt, so they had to fall back, wounded and worn out. The Gotalanders started complaining and thought this was hard to put up with, but the Swedes kept coming out on to the fortress wall, jeering and ridiculing them and calling them cowards. They brought out furs, silk, and lots of other valuable things to show off in front of them, and invited them to try and get the stuff. King Hrolf asked his brother Ketil what he thought of the progress they were making.

Ketil said he was finding it heavy going. 'I think the Swedish King's pissing a bit hot on us,' he said.

Hrolf said something more than idle chat was needed.

They stayed there for over a fortnight, and then Asmund said to Hrolf, 'We've been attacking this stronghold for a long time, and every day we've suffered heavy casualties without getting any nearer to what we're after. We've lost a good many, and there's a lot of men wounded. We expect you to give us advice that's going to be some use to us, sir, otherwise your men want to get out of here, since all we get for our efforts are insults and ridicule.'

King Hrolf said, 'I can't see how the town can be taken. Still, let's have another try. We'll go into the forest and gather loads of timber, then use it for making platforms built upon massive beams. Then we'll raise these platforms so high that men can stand up under them to support the pillars beneath. For this we'll have to pick our strongest men. The others are to get digging-tools and dig a hole through the wall, and that's how we'll try to get inside the fortress.' Everybody thought this a great idea, and when everything was ready, they brought the platform up to the fortress. It was so sturdily built the men under it weren't harmed either by the stones or the pitch.

When King Thorberg found out about this trick, he ran off with all his men into an underground passage that led from the stronghold, and so he and his men got away into the forest. King Hrolf marched with all his army into the stronghold, but by the time they got there everybody was gone. They thought it very peculiar that they couldn't see anybody in any of the houses, since in every house food and drink stood ready and clothes and jewels were lying all around.

Ketil said, 'This must be a feeble-hearted king to run away from all these precious things and leave this food and drink ready for his enemies. We've been rewarded for all our troubles sure enough, so first let's drink and eat here, and then divide the loot between us.'

King Hrolf listened to what he said. 'Now you're swallowing the bait intended for you,' said Hrolf, 'thinking more about filling your belly than capturing the King. I want nobody loafing around here, otherwise the King might get away. We'll have to make a thorough search to see if we can find any underground escape route.'

They did as the King told them, and in the end they found the passage going down from the fortress. Hrolf was the first in, and then the rest followed, one after another. They kept going and came up to find themselves in a forest. The Swedish King was there with all his retainers, and right away they began fighting. King Hrolf put up a good brave fight, as did all his blood-brothers. The Swedish King fought bravely too, and his followers, for they were all hard men and there were more of them than there were on the other side. When the blood-brothers came face to face with the Swedes they clashed fiercely and a good many Swedes were killed. The Swedish King kept urging his men on angrily and said they were useless followers if they couldn't ward off such a petty king. King Thorberg himself was putting up a spirited fight and with his warriors' help he put down a good many men. All the same, the battle was soon going badly for the Swedes.

King Hrolf had a word with his brother Ketil. 'I want you to start moving against this Swedish king and take him captive if you can. But you mustn't use weapons on him, for it's a cowardly thing to wound a woman with weapons.'

Ketil promised to do his best. Then the Swedes were routed. Ketil got so close he was able to bang the Swedish King on the backside with the flat of his sword. 'Lady,' he said, 'here's how we cure your itching crutch. That's what I call a dirty stroke!'

The King said, 'This stroke won't bring you any honour,' and then she hit Ketil with her axe under the ear so hard he was knocked head over heels. 'This is how we usually beat our dogs when they bark too loud,' she said.

Ketil jumped to his feet looking for revenge, but just then

King Hrolf came up and laid hands on King Thorberg. 'Lay down your weapons, sir,' said Hrolf, 'you're in my hands now. I'll spare the lives of all your men if you promise to do as your father says.'

The King of the Swedes said, 'I take it, King Hrolf, that you think you've got us all in your power, but it won't bring you any credit to force us into anything against our will.'

King Hrolf said, 'Look, sir, now we've met like this, I can only think of your honour. I'm going to ask your father to settle the whole issue, and if he's the one to judge between us, everybody will agree about the safety of your dignity and honour.'

The Swedish King said, 'What a shrewd and patient man you are! Most people would have made up their minds to force us to do what they wanted if they'd found themselves in your position, and got their own back for what we've done. Now that we know we're all in your power, we're going to accept your offer and get out of this prison right away. Like any gentlemen who've been defeated and overcome, we want to invite you, King Hrolf, with all your troops to take things easy and feast away to repay you for sparing the lives of our men. We'll ride straightaway now to Uppsala with all the survivors amongst our leading men, to see our father, King Eirik, and get some sound advice; it's fitting that we should follow his counsel.'

The two Kings sealed their agreement with firm guarantees, then King Hrolf turned back to the stronghold, where he enjoyed a three-day feast: but the Swedish King rode over to Uppsala with all his retinue. When he arrived there, he went before his father, King Eirik, laid the shield on the floor at his feet, took the helmet from his head, bowed to him, and said, 'Dear father, I've just been chased out of the kingdom you gave me and the reason is this – strong fighting-men have beaten me; so you can make whatever arrangements you like about my marriage.'

The King said, 'We'd be very pleased if you'd stop this fighting and turn to feminine matters in your mother's boudoir. After that, we'd like to marry you to King Hrolf Gautreksson, because we haven't come across his equal anywhere in Scandinavia.'

His daughter said, 'We'd never come to you for guidance without accepting your advice.'

She went over to the boudoir, handed her weapons over to King Eirik, and began working at embroidery with her mother. She was the loveliest, most polished and courteous woman in the whole of Europe, intelligent, popular, eloquent and the best of advisers, but imperious too.

CHAPTER 14

Wedding-feast

AFTERWARDS KING EIRIK sent messengers to King Hrolf to invite him and his troops to a feast. Hrolf wasted no time and hurried over to Uppsala. When King Eirik heard King Hrolf had arrived, he set out to meet him with all his retainers, led him into the palace and seated him on the throne beside his own seat, with Hrolf's blood-brothers on the other side of him. They started drinking and enjoying themselves, then began to discuss their private matters, in which they reached complete agreement. After that, King Eirik had his daughter called into the hall. As soon as she received word from her father, she put on all her finest things and went into the hall with her mother and a good many other noble women. When King Eirik saw his daughter coming into the hall, he stood up to meet her and led her to the seat just beside him, with his Queen on her other hand, and then all the other women in the party.

After the Kings had been drinking for some time, King Hrolf made a proposal of marriage in the hearing of the young woman, and there's no need to make a long story out of it, she was betrothed to him there and then. After that they swelled the feast, inviting a huge crowd from all over Sweden. It was a magnificent celebration and lasted for a fortnight. When it was finished King Eirik gave all the important people splendid gifts and treated them with the best good will, after which everyone went back home with the cheerful approval of King Eirik. King Hrolf stayed behind in Sweden with his bride, and they came to love each other very dearly.

King Hrolf sent Ketil, his brother, to Gotaland to take over the country. Ingjald went back to Denmark to his father. King Hrolf took charge of the kingdom his wife had ruled over, and everyone settled down in peace, each one in the place where he happened to be.

69

CHAPTER 15

Fighting

I N   T H E   S P R I N G, messengers from Denmark came to King
Hrolf to tell him that Hring was dead and that Ingjald wanted
Hrolf to come for a visit and celebrate a funeral feast for his
foster-father. As soon as King Hrolf heard the news, he started
making preparations for the journey, along with his blood-
brother Asmund. When they were ready, they sailed to Denmark
with two ships well-equipped with weapons and manned with
good crews. Ketil joined them with a single finely appointed
ship, and they sailed up to Zealand, anchoring to leeward of
some island late one day, where they put up the awnings.

King Hrolf went ashore with a number of men, and on the
other side of the island they saw five ships lying abreast. Four
were longships, and the fifth a huge dragon-head so impressive
the King thought he'd never seen a finer one. All these ships had
black awnings over them.

The King said, 'Who's the captain of this magnificent dragon-
ship, I wonder? I've never seen any ship I'd rather have.'

Asmund said, 'True enough it's a splendid ship in every way,
and fit for a king, but I think its owner isn't going to be at all
easy to beat, and he's one who thinks rather highly of himself.'

'Do you know who owns this dragon?' asked the King.

'He's called Grimar Grimolfsson, and he's a very great viking
indeed,' said Asmund. 'He stays aboard his warships summer
and winter. He's a big ugly man to look at, but he's even more

unpleasant to meet. Iron can't bite him, nor any of his eleven companions. They all eat raw meat and drink blood, and they've been rightly described as trolls rather than men. One summer we met near the Hebrides, I myself with ten ships, every one of them well manned, and they with five. We fought that day, and the matter didn't take long to decide between us: all my men were killed, I got away by diving into the sea, and that's the roughest treatment I've ever had to endure.'

'Do you think there's any sense in fighting them with the troops we have?' asked the King.

Asmund said that was up to him. 'But if we're going to win, we'll have to put our trust in your good luck,' he said.

Ketil was very keen that they should attack, and said it would be a good test of their skill at earning fame and loot.

King Hrolf said, 'Seeing they're evil and greedy men, and since they've got the one treasure I want for myself, let's get ready, let's load our ships with stones.'

They did as the King ordered, and made all the preparations they could. The King told some of his men to go ashore to the island and cut themselves heavy clubs. Then they armed themselves, and rowed softly towards the enemy. It's said that Grimar's ships were all lying abreast, with the long-ships nearest the island, and the dragon-ship to seaward. There was some distance between the ships and the island, so Hrolf and his men made first for the long-ships to see if they could take them before they got to the dragon. 'I think we can win if our men don't have to reckon with the long-ships on the other side when they attack the dragon-ship.'

The King told them to put up a good fight, now that the others were least expecting it, and make sure they dealt quickly with the enemy; he told them not to shout, but to go quietly, and they did as he said. It was pitch dark, with thick fog, and the crews of the long-ships knew nothing till the awnings were swept aside and they themselves were attacked with stones and weapons. They all sprang to their feet and tried bravely to fight back, for they had their arms at the ready. But before they could manage to form up properly to defend themselves, they'd received heavy casualties, and not long after the fighting started, King Hrolf boarded one of the ships. Soon a good number of men were dead, and Hrolf's men had cleared the first ship completely. Some of the vikings were killed, others jumped into the sea and were drowned. Three of the ships were cleared so completely that not a single man on board survived.

Then Grimar woke up and ordered his men on the dragon-ship to attack. This resulted in a lot of shouting and yelling, with everybody egging the others on.

King Hrolf said to his brother Ketil, 'You attack the remaining long-ship while Asmund and I make for the dragon-ship.'

Ketil said he'd do that, and now King Hrolf and Asmund laid their ships on either side of the dragon. They'd only lost a few men and the odds were in their favour.

Grimar stood up on the dragon-ship and asked, 'Who're these bold ones attacking us?'

King Hrolf said, 'If you really want to know, my name's Hrolf Gautreksson, and there's another called Asmund, a king's son from Scotland.'

Grimar said, 'We've met already, and the last time we parted he didn't seem to mind taking leave of us. We chased him overboard wounded, after we'd killed every one of his crew, but I suppose he must have forgotten it by now.'

Asmund said, 'Before the day's out, you'll find it hasn't slipped my memory.'

Grimar said, 'Your threats don't really frighten us much. Still, we know King Hrolf's famous for his courage, and we're going to make him an offer we've never made any-one before. It would be a great pity for a man like you to be killed, so here's our offer, King Hrolf. You can walk ashore to the island there with all your men fully armed and clothed, though I'm taking everything else you have here in compensation for the men of mine you've killed; and even so that's all too little. I've never made any man such a generous offer since I started my fighting career.'

When Hrolf had listened to these words, he said, 'This seems a very handsome offer. But there's nothing to suggest we're at your mercy or that you're in a better position to dictate terms to us than we are to you, so we're not going to throw our money away.'

Grimar said, 'I can see now you're not as smart a man as we thought, you don't even want to save your own skin. I'm telling you, this will be the last day of your life if you insist on fighting me. I'd have thought you'd want to live longer, for other people's sake, since they say you're a brave and popular man. That's why I wanted to be more generous to you than to anyone else. I thought it would add to my credit if I showed you more mercy than you deserved.'

King Hrolf said, 'You'll have no thanks from us over this, so

73

be quick and get yourself ready, we'll see which of us will be making the offers by the time evening comes on. As a matter of fact we've done your men a bit of damage already, and it's time you got your own back.'

'Now you've made a choice you'll always be sorry for, and you'll get what you deserve,' said Grimar.

Then a rough and angry battle started. Grimar and his men were tough and unflinching and so keen that Hrolf's men could only just manage to fend them off. They were finding it very hard to board the dragon-ship, too, because it was as high as a castle, and the defenders were strong and skilful. From up there, they could easily deal with the attackers, and iron couldn't bite into any of the twelve of them, just as Asmund had said. Hrolf's men were beginning to go down from weariness and wounds.

The story goes that Ketil Gautreksson laid his vessel alongside the one remaining long-ship. The captain of it was called Forni, the most courageous of men. Now each threw himself against the other, and a bitter struggle began. Ketil went for him hard and tried to board the ship with his men, and so the battle raged till at last he confronted Forni and killed him, and after that they slaughtered every man on board. Ketil's men thought highly of him for this. Then they made for the dragon-ship; and when the brothers met, Ketil asked Hrolf how he was getting on. King Hrolf wasn't very talkative, but he did say it wasn't a situation he'd put up with much longer, for these were real devils they were up against. He told Ketil to row out to the island, where there were plenty of big trees, and fetch some. Ketil did as he was asked, and had it done in no time.

When he got back, the King had the great trees laid against one side of the dragon-ship to make it tilt over. When Hrolf's party boarded the dragon-ship, the defenders started going down against the stones and weapons, and soon Grimar and his men were losing the battle. King Hrolf made his way aft along the deck striking to right and left with a huge club. Asmund and Ketil followed closely on his heels, and one after another the vikings went down. The King's force outnumbered theirs and Grimar's men kept falling till there were only twelve left standing, Grimar himself and his champions. Hrolf's men tried rushing them and began to pound them with clubs. When Grimar realised he'd lost, he jumped overboard and began swimming underwater. Asmund, who was standing close by, dived in after him and followed him to the island. King Hrolf saw this, and set out at once swimming towards the land to help Asmund so that he wouldn't have to fight Grimar single-handed. When Asmund got ashore, Grimar was there waiting and hurled a stone at him. Asmund dived underwater to dodge it, then came up again, and just as Grimar was going to throw another rock at him, the viking found himself knocked flat with a club. That was Hrolf who'd just turned up, and he kept hitting away at Grimar till he was dead. When Hrolf and Asmund came back on board the dragon-ship, they found Ketil had won it for them completely. Then they set to work, and cleared the decks, throwing all the dead overboard, and after that they went ashore to dress their wounds. They were tired and cut about, and many were dead. They spent several days there. The King was only slightly hurt, but Asmund and Ketil were badly wounded.

Afterwards they got ready to leave. They took the dragon-ship Grimar had owned but could hardly manage it for lack of hands, and left all the other ships behind. They reached Denmark, and when Ingjald heard that Hrolf had arrived, he invited him to the banquet he'd already prepared, the funeral feast in his father's honour. They celebrated Hring's funeral feast together in grand style, and nothing was so much a topic of conversation as the killing of Grimar and his men, for everybody thought it a great triumph. After the feast King Hrolf summoned people to a great assembly, and there Ingjald was made King over the whole of Denmark in succession to his father. He took up residence there and governed the land in the way King Hrolf had advised him. Then King Hrolf set out from Denmark bearing the magnificent gifts King Ingjald had honoured him with. He sailed on his way till he got back safe and sound to Sweden, but Ingjald stayed behind quietly in Denmark; they'd parted the best of friends. Ketil went back to Gotaland and there he lived in peace.

King Hrolf resided at Uppsala most of the time, for he and his father-in-law were on excellent terms. Hrolf spent a great deal of money to have Grimar's dragon-ship fitted out again and had it all painted above the sea-line in various shades: yellow, red, green, blue, black, and multi-coloured. The dragon-head he had decorated with gold, and also the headpiece and the bows and beams were inlaid with gold wherever it was thought to be an improvement. So she became the most elegant of all ships, surpassing every other vessel in the same way as King Hrolf himself was thought to surpass other chieftains throughout Scandinavia. He gained a widespread reputation as a wise ruler, and a lot of important people came to visit him, some even offering him their loyalty and allegiance. At that time, we've been told, there wasn't a ship manned with more famous warriors than Grimar's old dragon-ship, though we don't know the names of these warriors or any stories about them.

King Hrolf was in Sweden throughout that year living in great style with plenty of merry-making. Queen Thornbjorg loved him very much, and he discovered how very intelligent she was, in every way an exceptional woman. Asmund stayed with the King and was very highly thought of. He proved himself a brave and sturdy fighter, and the King considered him the best of his men. King Hrolf reigned over one third of Sweden, and every summer he used to go abroad looking for reputation and riches. The summer after his encounter with Grimar he went on a viking expedition, harried in many parts of Western Europe, and won a great deal of loot and fame. In the autumn he went back to Sweden, and there he stayed quietly over winter.

CHAPTER 16

King Halfdan

AT THAT TIME the ruler of Russia was a King called Halfdan, a wise man and well-liked. He had a beautiful daughter called Alof, thought to be the best match in Russia and even further afield, and he loved her very dearly.

There was a man called Thorir, King Halfdan's chief counsellor, a tall strong man, nicknamed Iron-Shield. He'd been in charge of the defences for a long time.

King Halfdan had twelve berserks. They were hard, wicked men, and iron couldn't bite into any of them. Two of them are mentioned by name, two brothers, one called Hrosskel, and the other Horse-Head. It's said of them they could wade through fire, and of their own free will they used to walk right into weapons when the berserks' fury came over them. They used to butcher men and cattle and everything that came their way and didn't give an inch, sparing nobody as long as the fury lasted. But once the rage had left them they were so weak they'd barely half their normal strength and were just as feeble as people who've been lying sick in bed. This weakness lasted for about a day. King Halfdan put a great deal of trust in their fighting power, and no king dared to attack him.

Halfdan was very fond of his daughter, and even though kings themselves asked to marry her, they were all chased off by the scoffing and jeering of the berserks, and were very glad to get away from these insults. This made the princess so choosy she wouldn't say yes to anyone who wanted her, so they all got tired of her answers, and kept out of her way.

CHAPTER 17

Ketil's proposal

ONE DAY QUEEN THORNBJORG said to King Hrolf, 'What do you plan to do this summer?'

The King replied, 'I'm going to plunder.'

'Have you heard anything about the travels of your brother Ketil?' she asked.

He said he hadn't. 'Can you tell us anything about him?'

'I've been told Ketil has gone east to Russia,' she said, 'to ask for King Halfdan's daughter. According to the news I've had, he went there with two ships, and walked into the King's palace with eleven other men. I understand he stated his business clearly and fluently enough and pleaded his case in a long eloquent speech, but the answers he got from the King and the young lady didn't exactly make him feel honoured, and then the berserks jumped to their feet screaming and shouting, and chased them out of the hall with howls and screeches like nothing they'd ever heard before. They were all of them beaten and hurt and had their legs to thank for saving them. That's the news we've heard. And we've been told that Ketil feels as dissatisfied now with the outcome of his expedition as he felt about you after the first visit you paid us. His trip's even more disgraceful. He'll soon be looking for you to ask you to help him revenge this humiliation.'

King Hrolf said, 'It's not exactly easy to talk sense to a man like him, so wild and headstrong. It'll do him good to suffer a bit through his own stubbornness, because he never pays any heed to what we tell him.'

She said he shouldn't talk like that, as helping one's brother was a really pressing business. With that they dropped the subject.

Soon afterwards Ketil came to see King Hrolf and told him in detail about all the humiliation he'd suffered in Russia.

King Hrolf told him this was just what he could have expected. 'You try to win at everything with nothing but your enthusiasm.'

Ketil asked King Hrolf to join him on this expedition. 'I don't think I've enough power to set right this insult I've had to endure,' said Ketil.

He was in a furious temper but the King told him his head-strong and empty talk wouldn't get him anywhere. 'I think it's going to prove a hard business to take vengeance on the people we're up against. We're going to need plenty of men and all our courage. First go back home to your kingdom and gather ships and men, then send word to King Ingjald in Denmark and ask him to do the same. Next summer you're both to come here, and we'll work out what's the wisest course for us to take.'

Afterwards Ketil went back home to his kingdom. The three leaders kept to the plan and started preparing for the expedition.

CHAPTER 18

To Russia

THE STORY GOES that after the winter had passed and summer had come, Ketil and Ingjald arrived in Sweden with forty ships, well-manned and equipped with fine weapons. King Hrolf had thirty ships ready, apart from his dragon-ship. All these ships were fitted out for real warfare and manned with first-rate crews. They waited for a favourable wind. King Hrolf asked his Queen what she thought of the expedition and how it would turn out. She said she thought things would go well with them, though she'd dreamed they'd find themselves in hot water before the affair was over, and their manhood would be thoroughly tested.

As soon as the wind blew favourably, each hoisted whatever sail he was equipped with, but at first the breeze was rather too gentle. King Hrolf was the last to be ready, and the dragon-ship moved slowly, as it needed a strong wind. They sailed on their way to Russia, and after a while a gale blew up, and then the dragon-ship began catching up with the rest of the fleet. The gale blew stronger and stronger, and the King told his men to link the ships together and see if this would make them more secure. But as they were trying to do that, the gale became so fierce that all the ships were driven apart. They were forced to reef their sails and let the ships drift. Then the gale turned into a foul northwesterly, and as it was impossible to drift any longer, they used just a single sail. The gale blew harder and harder

F   81

until the rigging fell apart, mainstays and braces were torn to shreds, a great sea swamped them, and hardly anyone expected to come out of it alive. When the storm was at its worst, King Hrolf's dragon-ship was driven away from the rest of the fleet up to some island, but it had a safe harbour, and the ship was manned with a staunch crew, so they made land safely. Late in the evening the wind dropped a little and the weather improved. King Hrolf said he wanted to go ashore onto the island to find out whether there was anything new to see. Asmund and ten other men went with him, but Hrolf told the rest to wait at the ships till noon the following day, unless he contacted them sooner.

Then they landed on the island, which was large and wooded. When they'd gone a little way, they came upon a house so big and strongly built, it seemed to them they'd never seen a place so high: the door was shut, and the King told his men to open it. One after another they threw themselves at the door, but no-one could budge it.

The King said, 'The man who usually opens this door must have some power to his paws. I'm going to see whether I can manage it.'

Then he went up to the door and pushed it open with one hand. The others came inside and started looking around; there was a fire burning there, and they kindled a firebrand and carried it through the house. They saw plenty of goods there of all kinds, and a fine bed made up. It was immense. When the King lay down on it it was so enormous, another man just as tall could stretch out sole to sole without covering the full length of the bed. Obviously the owner was no midget. In front of the bed stood a column supporting the roof-beam. A massive sword was suspended from it, but so high off the ground the King couldn't get anywhere near it.

King Hrolf said, 'What about spending the night here and waiting for the master of the house? Then we could find out how hospitable he is. Or would you rather go back to the ships and not risk meeting him?'

They told him to do as he liked, but added they weren't too keen to stay.

The King said, 'I'm inclined to wait for the householder, but it could be he'll think there's too many of us, and he may be a bit put out by so many visitors, so we'd better split up. Four men had better go down to the ship, and Asmund and I will stay here with the other four. You can tell the crew what's keeping us here, and if we don't get back to the ship before dawn, go on your way. There'd be no point in waiting, and I don't think it's worth attacking this man with a big force, because he'll be able to kill a lot of men as easily as a few if he's as powerful as I'm inclined to think. It will mean a lot more to our people if you can get away and describe what you've seen, and tell them what happened to Hrolf Gautreksson and his companions. It seems quite possible to me that the owner of this house may have had something to do with our being here. He may want me to meet him, so that's why we'd better spend the night here.'

Then the men King Hrolf had chosen set out and got back to the ship without any trouble. They told the crew what they knew about the King's plans, and everyone was scared in case something might happen to him.

CHAPTER 19

The giant

NOW WE COME BACK to Hrolf and his men. When they were settled down in the house for the night, he said, 'I'd very much like to get that big sword hanging up there.'

'How can we do that?' asked Asmund.

'Climb up on to my shoulders,' said the King, 'and see if you can reach up for it.'

Asmund said, 'I think the sword's far too heavy for me to hold.'

'Steady yourself against the column with one hand, and try to ease the sword up a bit with the other,' said the King, 'and when you feel it's free, let it slide down the column of its own weight. Then I can get hold of it.'

Asmund did as the King told him, climbed on to his shoulders, and pushed the sword upwards, and the king was able to get it.

The evening passed. Then they heard a loud din outside, and a man came into the house. That was when they stopped wondering why the hall was so enormous, because the newcomer was a massive giant, whose like they'd never seen before. He wasn't all that ugly to look at – in spite, that is, of his enormous features. He was well-dressed, and carried a grizzly bear on his back and a great bow in his hand. He looked tired out, so they assumed he must have walked some distance. The giant went up to the fire at the other end and threw the bear down on the floor. King Hrolf greeted him, but he paid no attention. Then he set to and started carving the bear up into pieces neatly and quickly, put the cauldron on and cooked the meat. Next he put up the table, spread a cloth on it, and laid out food and drink. Everybody thought this extremely well done. After that he settled down to his food, and ate and drank well, and when he'd had enough, he gathered together all that was left.

The story goes that he laid the table a second time, even more elegantly, and produced wash-basins and clean towels. Then he said, 'You must have been thinking I'm not a very hospitable man. But come to the table now, King Hrolf, and take a meal with your men. I'm not so mean that I grudge food to anyone who spends a night here, even to people less distinguished than yourself. You're a very famous man. Those great exploits of yours mark you out from all other kings.'

King Hrolf said, 'This is a kind and generous offer, and it proves you a big-hearted man, not just in this but in other things too. All the same, we'd plenty to eat and drink before we left the ship, so we don't need anything just now. What's your name, by the way?'

'My name's Grimnir,' he said, 'and I'm the son of Grimolf and brother of that Grimar you killed. You took a lot of treasure from him that I think belongs to me. Of course you don't deserve any kindness from me, and you'll not get it either. Even if you had your whole force with you, you couldn't ever get away from here, but I don't propose to scare you from my table. It was I who caused the fierce gale you ran into. I sent it against you and Asmund till the dragon-ship drifted away from the rest of the fleet. I didn't think the other ships worth much, and they've reached their destination because I gave them a good wind. But now that you and your crew have arrived here safe and sound with the dragon-ship, I'm never going to let you get away, for it's the best ship in all your fleet. Another thing, I'm going to take harsh revenge for my brother, but not with axe or sword, because a death from my weapons would be too good for you. I'm going to spare your life and Asmund's overnight to think up some torture for you that'll really put your courage to the test. As soon as I could see you'd been separated from your fleet, I gave them a good wind, and now they've got to where they wanted to go. I didn't want to be bothered by a crowd of your men.'

The giant had stuck an iron rod into the fire, forked at the end, so that it was like two separate irons. It was a vicious-looking weapon.

'I'd no idea that my blows had struck you so near home,' said King Hrolf, 'but, as the saying goes, "Everything has its price and compensation", and this should apply too in your case. You'll be willing to take compensation for your brother?'

'You must be frightened now, poor fellow, and that's just what I'd expected,' said the giant. 'Now I'm going to show you a little trick I sometimes perform for small boys when they pay me a visit.'

With that he pulled up the iron fork, drove the two prongs

into two of the king's men, and threw their bodies into the fire. Then he ran the fork into two others and threw them dead into the fire in the same way. Next he started shaking the fork so that you'd have thought it had four prongs.

Then he said, 'There's no need for you to be so scared now, my lord, you'll be given a longer and nastier torture in the morning.'

'It's always best to put off anything unpleasant,' said the King, 'and I find your little sport very entertaining – just as I will any other trick you think up.'

'There's some furs on the bench over there,' said the giant, 'you can put them under you to sleep on. I'm a very light sleeper, and I don't want to be disturbed by any noise from you.'

King Hrolf said, 'We'll be lying here by the fire with the furs under us. We'll soon be asleep.'

'You're a lot less scared than I expected, if you can go to sleep now,' said the giant. Then he slammed the door. 'Now I've made sure you're not getting out of my house,' he said.

King Hrolf said, 'We're not going to try. With a gracious host like you it seems best to do everything we're told.'

'Take it from me,' said the giant, 'it'll be best for you to lie quietly and not disturb me at all.' And that's what they said they'd do.

So now they all lay down to rest. The giant was tired and soon fell asleep.

'What do you think of your chances now, Asmund?' said King Hrolf.

'They've seldom been worse,' said Asmund. 'I think this

troll's going to be very hard to deal with, and there's no easy way out.'

The King said, 'This enemy's never going to beat us, we've a different destiny.'

Then he picked up a log and struck it against the wall. The giant woke up and told them to be quiet – 'or else I'll knock you dead with my fist.'

The giant fell asleep again, and again King Hrolf picked up the log and banged it. The giant turned over on the other side, but didn't wake up or speak to them, and was soon sound asleep again. The King banged with the log a third time, and harder than ever, but the giant didn't stir.

'We'd better go carefully now,' said King Hrolf. 'First I want to get hold of the sword, because I think it's likely it will bite into the giant. So let's go about it just as we did earlier this evening.'

They did as he suggested, and Hrolf managed to get the sword. 'Now I think things are beginning to look up a bit, and we must be very careful,' he said. 'You're to keep the giant's iron fork in the fire until it's red hot, and then I want you to drive it right into the giant's eyes, just as I thrust the sword into him. If anything goes wrong, we'd better run for it to the back of the house.'

King Hrolf drew the sword, picked up a log, and walked boldly up to the bed; he pulled the bedclothes off and the giant's troll-like features now stood revealed. The King thrust the sword into the left armpit so hard it went right through the body, and at the same time Asmund drove the iron fork into the giant's eyes. Then they ran away from the bed, and King Hrolf flung a log towards the door; it landed on a pile of firewood and made a loud clatter. The giant leapt to his feet, rushed to the door and groped about him in all directions, hoping to catch and crush them without mercy, but he collapsed from his terrible wounds with a great crash and smashed against the door so heavily it was shattered into little pieces. They went up to him and began beating him with heavy logs until he was quite dead, though he took a lot of killing, and then they dragged the body out of the house. All the same, they had to cut it limb from limb before they could get it out.

It was now early in the morning, and away they went. They'd only gone a short distance when they saw the rest of the crew coming towards them with their weapons rattling. The crew were delighted to see their King in good shape, because they'd made up their minds, if necessary, to go against the giant and avenge their lord, for they'd no wish to live if their King had been killed. They took a great deal of loot from the house, including a good many precious things. King Hrolf took the giant's sword, but it was so big Hrolf was the only one who could handle it, and even he found it rather heavy.

CHAPTER 20

In Russia

AFTER THIS EXPLOIT, they put out to sea and sailed before a favourable wind to Russia. Early in the morning they made land near the royal residence. The rest of their troops were already there, and everybody was happy at this reunion. Ketil and his men had just arrived. They enquired about Hrolf's voyage, and he told them the whole story. They thought he'd proved his good luck and what a great man he was too, and everyone praised his voyage and his exploits. Ketil asked King Hrolf if they shouldn't go to war right away and attack King Halfdan.

Hrolf said he was against the idea. 'I'm sending messengers to the King to tell him I've arrived and what my business is. I want you, Asmund, to go on this errand for me. Tell King Halfdan that if he refuses to have my brother as his son-in-law, he can reckon on open war between us. We'll give the King a fortnight to gather forces and get ready for battle, but we're going to win that woman for Ketil.'

Asmund set off with a number of men, and came to the King's hall where the King and his retainers were sitting at table having a good time. Asmund ignored the doorkeepers and walked straight into the hall. He came before the King and delivered the message firmly and fluently, just as King Hrolf had expected he would.

'We've been told King Hrolf's a remarkable man,' King

Halfdan replied, 'but since we've already rejected Ketil's proposal, we don't think it proper to accept it now, though you've brought a larger force this time than Ketil did. We're taking the other choice and mean to fight, particularly since King Hrolf has made us such a kind offer of time to gather forces.'

Then Thorir Iron-Shield, the King's chief counsellor, spoke: 'My advice, my lord, is this: don't fight King Hrolf, because he'll prove too much for you. Your daughter will be well-married if Ketil gets her, he's a tough, courageous man. It would strengthen your own position a lot to be allied to King Hrolf; we don't know of a more famous man in Northern Europe for energy, wisdom, and courage. You can take it from me, you'll lose face if you fight him, and if you won't take my advice, don't expect me to support you. I'm not going to carry my shield against King Hrolf.'

The twelve berserks sprang to their feet, and this is what their leader, Horse-Thief, said to Thorir: 'You're talking like a vile old coward, refusing your lord all the help you can give him without the courage to fight even a petty little king. After an outburst like that you don't deserve any honour from our lord, and even if the King hadn't a soul apart from us twelve berserks, he'd still send these men to Hell with all their supporters, and there'd be no survivors. I'm the one who's going to become King Halfdan's son-in-law, and I'll cut King Hrolf up into bits for ravens and eagles. You messengers had better clear out of here quick unless you want to be maimed and flogged. You can tell your King to expect a hard battle from us before King

Halfdan gives his daughter to the man we know to be in every way the puniest idiot we've ever heard of. It's incredible that he should dare try this a second time, after he'd been chased away from here and beaten like a dog at the sheep-fold.'

'When I look at you, Horse-Thief,' Asmund replied, 'I can see you're speaking with a doomed tongue, and all your companions are going to die soon too. King Hrolf wouldn't have anything to fear from you, even if you'd been men, and a lot less so when you bleat like gutless forest goats. You'll come to a bad end, and it's a stupid thing you're urging your King to do.'

With that Asmund walked out of the hall, but the berserks kept yelling and screaming after him and his men. The King told the berserks to be quiet and stop making these uncouth noises, adding that it was a manly business to deliver a message from one's king.

Asmund came back to King Hrolf with news of what had happened, that they could expect a battle. King Halfdan gathered forces, and in a few days he'd brought a great army. Both sides got themselves ready, and on the day appointed for the battle King Halfdan led his army against King Hrolf. The berserks were in the lead, some distance away from the rest of the troops, because they wanted to hold apart from other warriors on account of their strength and recklessness.

King Hrolf told Ingjald, Asmund, and Ketil to form up and meet King Halfdan, but said he wanted to tackle the berserks himself single-handed. They didn't think this very wise, but the King insisted on having his way and set out against the berserks alone.

When they met, the King asked, 'Who are these who think so highly of themselves they walk ahead of the king's own column?'

Horse-Thief gave his name, and Hrolf said, 'I know your family right enough. Your father, Hrosskel, was a close friend of my father King Gautrek, and they used to exchange gifts. Now that you're insisting on fighting me, I must tell you a little story to throw some light on your family background. One time, as often happened, your father came to Gotaland. My father gave him a good welcome and invited him to a feast, which he accepted. Your father stayed a long time, enjoying lavish hospitality. My father owned some valuable studhorses, big fine creatures: a splendid great dapple-grey stallion and four mares, and when your father left, King Gautrek gave him many fine gifts, including these horses. Your father was extremely pleased with these valuable presents, particularly the horses, and thanked King Gautrek eloquently. Then they parted, and your father went back home, taking the horses with him. He took great care of them and used to go and see them every day. It wasn't long before he began to grow less fond of the stallion than he'd been at first. People noticed too that he was thinking more of the mares, and one day when he came to the herd, what should he find but the stallion stabbed to death with a spear. Your father didn't seem to care about this, and everyone thought it a bit strange that he shouldn't feel the loss of such a fine horse. Afterwards your father started seeing the mares more often than before and stuck even closer to them. One of the mares, a fawn-coloured one, he thought the best of the lot. In the spring everyone who saw the fawn mare thought she was in foal, and in due course of time she gave birth. But it didn't turn out as people had expected, because she bore a boy, not a foal. Your father took the baby and had him reared – a big fine-looking boy – called him Horse-Thief, and said he was his son, so it's not strange you should think yourself so special seeing that you're the son of a mare. Your father had killed the stallion. I don't know whether he gave that mare any more sons, but I'm told he had another son called Horse-Head, sprung from horses too. You're all of you very like one another, so vile and inhuman you must all have been conceived in the same way.'

At this, all the berserks jumped to their feet howling and screaming, and all wanting to set on him at the same time. Hrolf drew the giant's sword and hit out first at the man in the lead. The sword went through their bodies as if it was cutting through water. None of the berserks had any protective armour, because they'd never been harmed by weapons before. The outcome was that King Hrolf killed every one of them, though he himself was hardly scratched.

Then he saw that the armies of King Halfdan and the blood-brothers were clashing. King Halfdan had a much larger force, but Hrolf turned to fight him. It was a long, hard battle, and the blood-brothers went at it busily. King Halfdan's army soon began to fall back before King Hrolf's attack, and a great number were killed there.

It's already been said that Thorir Iron-Shield wouldn't fight against King Hrolf when Halfdan chose to ignore his advice. The princess, who'd climbed to the top of the highest tower to watch the battle, saw how her father's best men were being

killed. She went back into the palace and into the hall where
Thorir Iron-Shield, her foster-father, was sitting alone on the
high seat muttering to himself.

She went up to him and said, 'Foster-father, the time's come
to go and help my father, I can see he needs it.'

Thorir looked at her but didn't say a word or get up, and she
went away.

A little later she came back to him, and said, 'Foster-father,
why are you sitting back and giving no help to my father when
he needs it so badly? It's a disgrace, and you'll be called a
coward for this. After all, you're his right-hand man, you've
had lots of gifts from him and he's always taken your advice
whenever you felt like giving it.'

He looked at her angrily but said nothing, still keeping to his
seat, and the girl went away thinking her foster-father must be
in an ugly mood. She went out to have another look at what was
happening, and saw King Halfdan's men retreating and King
Hrolf striking out to right and left.

She hesitated whether or not to go back once more to her
foster-father to plead with him, but at last she went up to him
boldly, put her arms round his neck and said, 'Dear foster-
father! I beg you, help my father, so that I won't be married
against my will. You've promised to grant me one request if I
ask you, and now I want you to go into battle and give my
father all the support you can. I know you'll fight well.'

Thorir Iron-Shield knocked the girl flat on the ground and
seemed so angry she didn't dare speak to him. Then as he sprang
to his feet she heard him fetch a deep groan. He seized his

weapons, put on his armour quickly with a practised hand, and ran to the battlefield, where there was plenty of killing going on and the fighting was fierce. Thorir went forward so hard that everything got pushed aside out of his way. A little later King Hrolf happened to look around and saw the troops under Ingjald and Ketil giving way, so he told Asmund to fight under his banner till he came back. Then he went over to the others. When the brothers met, the King asked how they were getting on.

Ketil said it was hard going. 'There's a new enemy turned up, so tough we can't do anything with him, he's more like a monster than a man.'

The King said, 'He's a man all right, though he may be a bit braver than the rest.'

The King started hitting out to right and left with the giant's sword, but he'd never met anyone so brave, strong, confident, and less ready to exchange life for death. Ketil followed up courageously, killing a good many men, and so the brothers forced their way through the enemy ranks. Then suddenly Thorir Iron-Shield vanished, and the King was able to straighten his line again. But when they'd been fighting for some time, Hrolf saw Asmund was giving way so he went back to his own banner and had it carried forward in a great onslaught. King Halfdan fought well, being a tough man in battle and a keen fighter, and he killed a good many. Then Thorir turned up there fighting hard, laying about him, and making short work of anyone trying to stop him. But when he saw King Hrolf, he moved off quickly over to Ketil and his men, fighting as

keenly as ever and killing one after another, and there was no
holding him.

The foster-brothers were losing the battle, and Ketil realised
this would never do, so he went over to King Hrolf and said to
him, 'I can't see why you haven't put an end to this monster
that's causing us all the damage. We'd have won long ago if we
hadn't this troll fighting against us. We've never known you to
lack courage and keep out of the thick of the fight before, but
this trouble-maker today's causing you to lose heart. Each of
you seems to be steering clear of the other. If you don't want to
destroy this man – if that's what he is – give me the giant's
sword, and see whether I back down when I get within reach
of him.'

The King said, 'You're a hard man all right, and you'd be
doing fine if you had the same amount of foresight. How do you
think you can fight with a weapon even I can hardly carry?'

Ketil said, 'Of course I know the sword's no use to me, but I
had to get you going somehow.'

The King joined Ketil and started fighting by his side, and it
was a rough, grimly-fought battle. Thorir Iron-Shield was there
to meet him, hitting always to right and left, and laying people
out in large numbers. The King turned against Thorir with a
small band of men, and a hard fight followed. The King realised
this would never do, but he could see Thorir obviously didn't
want to hurt him, because he kept backing away. The King got
so close to Thorir he hewed down the man standing in front of
him, and next he stretched out and killed the man standing
behind. After that someone dropped down just at the King's

feet so that he stumbled over him and nearly fell himself, then thrust the sword at Thorir and tried to steady himself. Thorir twisted quickly away from him, wrapping his clothes round himself as he went, and it wasn't long before the King couldn't see him anywhere—he seemed to have vanished from the battlefield.

The King urged his men forward, and turned himself to meet King Halfdan. It was obvious that wherever there was any fighting going on, all the enemy survivors were on the run. King Halfdan fled to the town with all those who'd escaped alive, but a large number had been killed. King Hrolf had lost a lot of men too, and told his wounded to go down to the ship. Then he asked Asmund to come with him, and they went into the forest, while the rest of the troops made their way to the ships.

Asmund said, 'What are you looking for here in this wood?'

The King said, 'At the height of the battle I gave a sword-cut to the big man who'd been killing so many of our men. I'd like to meet him again, and I think he went into this wood.'

Asmund said, 'Don't you think he's most likely dead from the wounds? I suppose you want to kill him?'

'Not at all,' said the King. 'I'd like to find him and heal him if I can, for I think I'd rather have just him on my side than any ten other men, however tough.'

Asmund said, 'This troll's probably walked into a cliff and won't ever be found.'

'That won't happen,' said the King, 'and I'm going to keep on looking for him.'

After they'd been walking through the wood for a while, they came to a clearing, and under a certain oak they saw a man lying in a pool of blood. He was deadly pale and his weapons were lying beside him.

The King went up to him and said, 'Who's this man lying here?'

'I recognise you all right, King Hrolf Gautreksson,' the man said, 'by your size and good looks. I suppose you must have come here to kill me, and you'll probably think you've plenty of reasons for that. I shan't hide my name from you: people call me Thorir Iron-Shield.'

'Have you been fighting us today and killing a lot of our men?' asked the King.

'I have that,' said Thorir, 'and I could have done you much more harm had I wanted to, but I knew King Halfdan would lose to you, and I didn't want to go into this battle, as I felt sure that one of us would be killed by the other. That's why I did my best to keep away from you; I thought your death would be a loss to your kingdom that no-one could make up for, so I didn't fight you wholeheartedly. And you didn't really mean to give me this wound.'

'You must be a really brave fighter,' said King Hrolf. 'Would you like me to spare your life?'

Thorir said, 'I don't think it makes very much difference now.'

'Are you badly hurt?' asked the King.

Thorir said it wasn't too serious: 'But I did get a scratch from your sword that's made me a mite stiffer than before, and I suppose it must be affecting me a bit.'

The King asked Thorir to show him the wound, and Thorir took off his clothes. The King saw the whole belly had been ripped open and the entrails were only held in place by the inner membrane.

The King said, 'You've got a nasty wound there, and it won't be easy to mend, but since your guts haven't fallen out I'll try to heal you, on condition you become my man, and serve and support me.'

Thorir said, 'If I'm to serve anyone, I'd choose you rather than anybody else. I'll accept my life only on condition you come to terms with King Halfdan and all his men, for he hasn't the power to fight you.'

The King said he'd do that if Halfdan fell into his power. After he'd cleaned the wound, he took a needle with silk thread and stitched it up. Then he applied all the best healing ointments, dressed the wound and did everything else he thought necessary. After that all the pain and smarting seemed to go away, and Thorir felt he could go almost anywhere if he'd a mind to. So then they went down to the ships and spent the night there.

Early in the morning King Hrolf briefed his troops and set out for the town. There was no resistance, and King Halfdan was taken prisoner. King Hrolf came to terms with him, as Thorir had requested, but stipulated that he alone should settle the whole issue between them. King Halfdan agreed to let Ketil marry his daughter. Then King Hrolf went back to his ships to have the wounded men seen to, and to bury the dead. King Halfdan prepared a feast, inviting a lot of important people in the land, and at the appointed time King Hrolf came to this feast with his men, and they all started drinking and enjoying themselves in good friendship and complete harmony. They carried on in splendid style for a week, and at this feast Ketil made Alof his wife, with her full consent and also her father's. King Halfdan gave her a great deal of gold, silver, and other precious things as her dowry. At this feast King Hrolf gave his brother the whole of Gotaland and with it the title of King.

When the feast was over, King Hrolf went away with all his followers, honoured by King Halfdan with many splendid gifts. One of the treasures was a superb drinking horn he called the Ring-Horn. It had this remarkable quality, that if someone was drinking from it, it rang out so loudly the sound could be heard a French mile away if the horn had some important news to foretell. But no-one could get a single draught from it if he didn't drink properly. A huge gold ring was on the point of the horn. Everybody thought it a treasure fit for a king. King Hrolf insisted on Thorir coming with him, and King Halfdan thought it a great loss to see him go. The two Kings parted the best of friends, and King Halfdan realised how far above other kings Hrolf really was. Everyone was very much impressed by the strength and resolution he'd shown when, singlehanded, he killed the twelve berserks who'd believed nothing was beyond their power and who'd never lost a battle.

They sailed away from Russia with the bride they'd won and all the other valuable things. When they got back home to Sweden everybody was delighted to see them. After they'd enjoyed a splendid welcoming feast, Ingjald went home to Denmark and Ketil to Gotaland, each to take charge of his kingdom and govern it with a great deal of skill and credit. But King Hrolf stayed behind in Sweden, and Asmund with him.

That same winter King Eirik of Sweden died, so King Hrolf took charge of the entire kingdom and became the sole ruler of Sweden, just as King Eirik had been. King Hrolf had a son by his wife and called him Gautrek. He was a big boy and showed early promise. Each of these kings reigned over their kingdoms in great peace and honour, and that's how it was for some years.

CHAPTER 21

The King of Ireland

THERE WAS A KING called Hrolf who ruled over Ireland, a great man for sacrifices, powerful, and very hard to deal with. He had an only daughter called Ingibjorg, an intelligent good-looking girl, considered the best match in Ireland. A good many reputable kings' sons had proposed to her, but her father wouldn't marry her to anyone. The suitors had tried both force and cunning, but Hrolf could see into the future, and with the help of his evil and depraved belief he knew about their coming beforehand, so he always had an invincible army to meet them even when they tried to take him by surprise. He himself was a great berserk in battle, and he'd killed many a warrior in single combat when he'd been challenged. Because of all this he got such a reputation, there wasn't a king who had any inclination to fight him, and for a long time he'd been left in peace. No king wanted to attack his land, because everybody was afraid of his ruthlessness.

The story goes that Asmund came one day to have a talk with King Hrolf Gautreksson. 'It's like this, sir, I'd like to settle down and get married. My father's getting on in years and I'm supposed to succeed to the throne when he dies.'

'Where do you plan to go for this, foster-brother?' said King Hrolf.

'There's a king ruling Ireland called Hrolf,' said Asmund, 'a very talented man with a clever, good-looking daughter called Ingibjorg. I'd like to get her as my wife, and with really firm backing from you I'm sure I could manage it.'

King Hrolf said, 'Surely you must have heard about King Hrolf. He's top-full of magic and sorcery, and nothing's going to take him by surprise. And Ireland's a difficult country for a foreign army to attack. It's thickly inhabited, and there are great shallows off the coast, so that you can't land except with small ships. And I've also heard some important people have asked for the hand of this girl already, and got nothing from the King but shame and humiliation. As you know, foster-brother, our wooings in the past haven't gone very smoothly, and we've had to undertake wars and battles, with heavy loss of life. Even when the kings aren't keen to fight us, the womenfolk move in and take up arms against us with all kinds of trickery, so we'd better find something easier to do than go against King Hrolf of Ireland. I think the Swedes, Danes, and Gotalanders will all agree with me, the time's come to stop this squandering on war and cut down the expenditure we run into every summer.'

Asmund could see the King was all against this, because he kept pointing out the snags involved in the expedition. He knew, of course, what a hard man King Hrolf of Ireland was to deal with, and what a rough handling he'd given all those who'd sought a marriage alliance with him. But Asmund could think of nothing else and kept pestering the King about it and asking him for support and advice, even if the King didn't want to go himself. The King said nothing would come of it apart from a great deal of killing. When Asmund realised how adamant the King was about it and how unwilling to listen to his case, he went to the Queen and asked her to plead on his behalf: he told her what he wanted and repeated his conversation with the King.

The Queen said she'd gladly do all she could for him. 'But I can't help you very much with this particular favour, because I can't think of any way you could keep your honour and your advantage when dealing with a man as evil as King Hrolf of Ireland, a harsh king with a vicious character. That's just what King Hrolf Gautreksson realises. Being a shrewd man, he can look into the future, and his guesses are never far from the mark.'

CHAPTER 22

Preparations

THE STORY GOES that King Hrolf and his Queen were having a conversation one day, and she asked him if he was refusing to support his blood-brother Asmund on that expedition to Ireland. He said it was true.

'That's very mean of you,' she said. 'There's nobody's honour you could better be adding to than his. Asmund's been your loyal follower for a long time and always served you like a gentleman. He's stood by your side on more than one dangerous expedition, he's shared with you good and bad alike, and always proved himself the bravest of men.'

The King said, 'Our wooings have never gone so well for us, even when we weren't up against hell-hounds like King Hrolf of Ireland, so we're putting an end to all these courtships. But if you must urge this affair so strongly, what plan have you in mind to give us any chance of success in our business?'

She said she'd no advice to offer, 'but if you make the ex-pedition, my lord, things will go according to your fate and your foresight. I suggest you take a small force on this campaign. I want you to leave Ketil and Ingjald behind and not to take any troops from their kingdoms, as they'd find that sort of levy a bit tiresome. I want Thorir Iron-Shield left here in charge of the defences while you're away. You and Asmund ought to go with no more than ten ships and a hundred men on each; but take the dragon-ship as well. I know sure enough that if

105

anything delays your return, Ketil and Ingjald aren't likely to wait around for long. I'd say that's how you're more likely to be avenged – should there be any need – as long as you've still got men like Ketil and Ingjald.'

So King Hrolf spoke to Asmund. 'Now that I'm joining you on this trip, blood-brother, then no matter what the outcome I'd like you to do me a favour in return. I've been told your father has a beautiful daughter called Margaret. I want you to leave any decision about her marriage in my hands.'

Asmund agreed gladly, and said he was sure the King would provide for her better than he could himself.

After that they started planning their expedition, and by midsummer all the ships and troops going with the King were ready. Thorir wanted to go with them, but the King wouldn't have it. So Thorir said that if he felt like it he'd go by himself after they'd left. He was unhappy that he wasn't free to do as he pleased, but added he wouldn't go with the King unless the King wanted him to. The King told him to rule and govern the land. Thorir said that, in his opinion, King Hrolf was going to need a good deal of extra help before he came back from this trip, and they parted rather abruptly.

King Hrolf had a second son by his wife, called Eirik. Hrolf's other son, Gautrek, was eleven years old when his father set out on this expedition.

CHAPTER 23

King Ælla of England

THE NEXT THING was that, as soon as they were ready, they set out from Sweden and sailed west across the sea. They made little headway because they ran into foul weather and adverse winds. Then there were dense fogs, so that they had a hard time of it and had to lie at anchor for long periods off islands and headlands. They kept coming across vikings, and what happened every time was that King Hrolf won the fight.

The story goes that they reached England late in the summer. The ruler there at the time was King Ælla, a famous and powerful king. When he heard that King Hrolf Gautreksson had landed there, he sent messengers along to invite him to a feast, bringing as many men as he pleased. King Hrolf told his men of the invitation and asked what they thought about going to the feast. They said it was up to him, so off he went with a hundred men.

It's said that King Ælla owned a certain creature so wild and savage it spared not a living thing it was set upon. A great strong lion it was, and it had been trained to harm no-one unless he'd opposed the King and the King wanted the beast to attack: but it was tame and quiet with the retainers and everyone else the King wanted to stay with him in peace. The King thought a lot of this animal, because whenever his land came under attack he had the lion set free, and within minutes it had slaughtered hundreds and hundreds of men. It defended the country so well that there wasn't a king thought himself strong enough to fight England once he knew about the lion.

There were two brothers staying at King Ælla's court, called Sigurd and Bard. They were both highly thought of, and it was they who watched and guarded the lion, which was usually shackled with strong iron chains. But these brothers were ruthless, malicious men. When they heard that King Hrolf had been invited with his retinue, Sigurd said, 'What can we do to make this king everybody loves so much lose his reputation? I don't care one bit for our King's honouring him like this.'

Bard said, 'I think we ought to go into the forest, right in their way, and take the lion with us, and when we see them coming we'll set it free. This king's not so tough that he can beat this creature, it's sure to kill him, and that would serve him right and please me.'

They took the lion into the forest and lay in wait there till they saw King Hrolf coming. They'd drugged the lion with wine and all sorts of strong drinks. Then they let the lion run free, and hid themselves.

CHAPTER 24

Death of a lion

MEANWHILE, KING HROLF had gone ashore and was on his way with his hundred men to meet King Ælla. They'd only travelled a short distance when they heard the trees creaking behind them and some terrible noises.

'Sir,' said Asmund, 'what's this noise we can hear?'

The King told his men to stand still and try to work out what it could be, but no-one had any idea except that everyone thought it a terrible thing to have to listen to.

The King said, 'They tell me the King of England owns a wild beast that's very hard to deal with. Maybe someone's not being entirely honest with us. Wait here while Asmund and I go and find out what's behind all these noises.'

So that's what they did. They'd only gone a little way when they saw the lion playing about in the wood. It was testing its strength by twisting its tail round the oak-trees and pulling them up by the roots. Then it caught the trees with its claws and threw them high up into the air, like a cat playing with a bird.

'Why's the monster going on like this?' asked Asmund.

'I think it must be out of its mind and crazy with drink,' said the King.

Asmund said, 'What with this devil, I can see we're not going to be able to finish our journey.'

'We'll have to think up a new plan,' said the King. 'There's a tall trunk just off the road where the wood's thickest. You climb that tree and stand up on top, and I'll keep out of sight and use you as bait for the creature. When the lion comes rushing up, jump over to the trees and I'll try to get at it. I think maybe the lion will get stuck in the trees as the wood's so dense there. You keep grunting loud like a pig, that's something the lion just can't stand. That's the way it's made, that's the only sound that frightens it.'

Asmund did as the King told him, and everything happened

as he'd said it would. When the lion saw the man it came rushing towards him, fierce and raging, running between the trees. Asmund did as he'd been told and kept grunting at the top of his voice. When the lion heard this noise, it stopped in its tracks, put its head between its legs and covered its ears as best it could, so as not to hear the grunting. Then King Hrolf came running forward, hewed at the lion with his sword and sliced clean through its back just in front of the loins. The lion died instantly.

When the brothers Sigurd and Bard saw this, they ran as quickly as they could back to the palace and told King Ælla all about the outrage, how King Hrolf had killed the beast everyone thought invincible. The King asked how this had happened, and they told the whole story. The King was in a great rage with them for what they'd done, and said it wasn't for them to try their luck against King Hrolf, and then he had them put in shackles. After that King Ælla set out to meet King Hrolf with a large following, saying it was quite likely King Hrolf would blame him for this treachery of the brothers.

After they'd killed the lion, Asmund and King Hrolf went back to their men. King Hrolf said, 'We'll carry on with our journey just as we'd planned, because I don't think King Ælla is behind this. But I suppose he'll think the lion's death a great loss, and I want to tell him all about it myself.'

They went on their way till they were out of the wood and saw a great crowd of well-armed men coming towards them. It seemed to them this spelt trouble.

King Hrolf said, 'This king's either full of tricks and treachery, and he's already made up his mind to kill us dishonestly, or else this wasn't his idea, some evil people are behind it who've done it to cause trouble between us, which seems to me just as likely. Act bravely, walk right towards them confidently and don't show any signs of fear, no matter whether these men mean to do us good or ill. If it comes to that, we'll die honourably rather than live in shame.'

They plucked up courage and said to hell with anyone who didn't do his best. They formed up, with King Hrolf leading the centre of the column and carrying the naked sword he'd taken from the giant, all very warlike.

When King Ælla saw this, he ordered the flag of peace to be hoisted, and rode himself to meet King Hrolf. King Ælla gave him a good welcome, and repeated his invitation. When King Hrolf saw how friendly King Ælla was, he accepted the offer gladly, so they all rode together into the town, where a great reception and a lavish feast awaited them.

The Kings started talking together, and King Hrolf said, 'A thing I must tell you, we've done you a lot of damage. I've killed an animal of yours and I've a feeling that this'll be a great loss to you. But I thought I was defending my very life, and that's why I had to do it, not out of any malice towards you. I want to offer you compensation for any inconvenience that you decide I've caused you.'

King Ælla said, 'In this you show, as usual, what a really wise man you are, offering compensation when others should be compensating you. And since you're not blaming this on our treachery, I want to hand over the men responsible for you to judge and punish.'

Then he sent for Sigurd and Bard. They were brought shackled before the Kings, and they described the whole plot in their own words. King Ælla asked King Hrolf to judge the case and decide how they should be put to death.

King Hrolf said, 'Whatever your own men do wrong, sir, ought to be judged by yourself. But if you'll do me a favour, I'd like to ask you to spare their lives and banish them from your land instead, as punishment for their treachery.'

'It's a fact,' said King Ælla, 'there aren't many kings to compare with you in magnanimity. I'm going to do just as you suggest.'

He had the brothers unshackled and gave them a ship and some money, and they went abroad, and now they're out of the story.

The Kings carried on with their talk. King Ælla asked King Hrolf about his travels, and Hrolf told him all about his plans. King Ælla said it was an expedition without much of a future, King Hrolf of Ireland being so very rough and hard to deal with. He warned King Hrolf not to persist in going there that summer and suggested he stay with a hundred men as his guests over the winter, and they could billet the rest of Hrolf's men somewhere in England not too far away. King Hrolf accepted this offer, and King Ælla took charge of all the arrangements and paid all the expenses. So King Hrolf and all his troops stayed on in England, enjoying themselves. King Ælla treated them very hospitably, and so time went by.

CHAPTER 25

The old hag

THE STORY GOES that King Hrolf and Asmund were out
walking in town one day to while away the time, and when
they turned back and started towards the hall, an old woman
on two crutches came up to them.

The old woman stuck up her nose in the air and said, 'Who
are these distinguished-looking men?' They told her.

The old woman said, 'So this is the famous King Hrolf
Gautreksson. Well, I'm pleased to meet you.'

'What did you want from King Hrolf?' asked the King.

'I must agree, what people say is true, you're the most
handsome and gentlemanly of kings, head and shoulders above
all the others. I'm hoping I might have the benefit of a bit of
advice from you.'

The King asked her what she wanted. She said, 'I've not got
much, I live alone in my house, except for my daughter, who
looks after me. She's a nice-looking girl, but now she's worse
than useless to me because there's a man trying to seduce her,
very much against my wishes, and she thinks of nothing but
him. He's a big, handsome fellow, but I don't care for him.
I'd like you to come and have a word with this man, sir, because
he's sure to stop bothering my daughter if you tell him to.'

King Hrolf said, 'Certainly, woman, I'll come one of these
days and see the fellow.'

The old woman showed them where she lived, and the King

went back to the palace, and some days went by. Then the King said to Asmund it was time to visit the old girl.

Asmund said, 'I think she's an evil old woman, and not to be trusted. I don't like her a bit.'

The King said it was important this man shouldn't bother the woman any longer, but Asmund said he didn't care if the man had both women. That day, after they'd been drinking, they went over to the old woman's house. The living-room was small, and they saw a pretty young woman sitting on the raised benches, and a tall brave-looking man beside her. He was fully armed and kept talking to the girl. The old hag sat in the corner under a cloak and a tattered priest's-robe. They greeted the King.

When the old hag realised the King had arrived, she started to her feet, grasped the two crutches and stepped down on to the floor. 'I beg you, sir,' she said, 'take vengeance for our shame, and kill this villain who's seducing my daughter and causing me so much misery.'

'Don't rush it, my dear,' said the King. 'Maybe you'll get your own way even if we take things easy.'

'No, that'll never do,' said the old woman, 'and they've caused me so much worry with this business, I'm not going to stand for it any longer now I've someone to help me.'

At that the old hag raised one of her crutches with the idea of hitting the young man on the ear, but he warded off the blow with his shield, and she hit the shield so hard that her crutch broke in two.

King Hrolf took hold of the old hag and said, 'Now that I'm here, you'd better let me put things right for you.'

He set her down on the seat beside him, and asked, 'Who's this man that's battling with the old woman?'

'My name's Grim,' he answered.

'What sort of a man are you?' asked the King.

'My father's called Thorir. He's a farmer and lives in a village not far from here.'

The King said, 'You're a fine-looking fellow. How often do you come to the old woman's house?'

He said he came there often. The King said, 'The old woman's been complaining to me that she thinks you're chatting too much to her daughter. She thinks the girl's making too little money out of her work, and it's the only source of income for the two of them. I want to ask you to stop annoying the old woman like this. It's no great matter for you, and it does you no credit to keep bothering her in this way. You'll have my thanks if I don't need to do any more about this than talk to you. I'll offer you a favour in return.'

'I hadn't meant to change my habit of coming and going,' said Grim, 'no matter who tried to stop me, but now that you've asked me, I'll do as you please. I'd have to wait a long time before anyone as noble as you made me a request, and I shan't wait long to ask you a favour in return. My wish is this, that you make me your retainer and let me come with you next summer. I've never taken part in a battle, so I'm curious to put myself to the test.'

'I'll grant you this gladly,' said the King. 'You look like a good man to me, and a lucky one, too. Come and join us next summer.'

Grim went outside, and they parted the best of friends.

Then the old woman got up and thanked the King for what he'd done. 'Could there be any king as obliging as you?' she asked. 'And, by the way, do you know the cure for old age?'

'I don't, and I can't imagine one,' said the King.

Asmund said, 'You often find something in a poor man's hut that you won't find in a king's palace. I know how to cure you of old age, if you care to try my remedy.'

She said she wanted it very much. 'Do you cure me in bed?'

He said, 'You come over to me, and I'll set about it my own way.'

The old woman threw away her crutch and went over to Asmund. He was carrying a wood-cutter's axe and told her to bow to him. She did as he asked, thinking he wanted to whisper something to her, but Asmund let fly at her neck with the axe, and sliced off her head.

'Now I've cured you of old age,' he said.

King Hrolf hadn't been paying any attention to their talk and looked at them just as her head was flying off. He was so angry at this he could hardly keep his hands off Asmund. The King said this was a vile, unspeakable crime, and they'd never recover from the shame and lasting disgrace of having killed a poor old woman in a foreign land. Asmund said he couldn't see what all the fuss was about, and this led to a bitter argument between them. With that they went back to the palace.

When they'd settled down at the drinking-table, King Ælla noticed that King Hrolf wasn't in a happy mood and asked at once what was the matter. King Hrolf told him the whole story and said this was a terrible misadventure.

Ælla told him not to worry. 'She was a nasty old hag, full of tricks and treachery and lies. We're well rid of her.'

Asmund said he'd never seen King Hrolf so angry over such a trifle.

CHAPTER 26

Two English earls

THE STORY GOES that certain great men in England started slandering King Hrolf Gautreksson and telling King Ælla lies, that Hrolf was plotting against him. The people behind the vicious talk were two earls and a number of important men. They said King Hrolf planned to take over the kingdom by any means at hand. King Ælla wouldn't believe this, though for some time they kept up a whispering campaign against Hrolf. But still the King continued to entertain King Hrolf just as before and said this must be a gross lie. However, in the end the king's suspicions were aroused, for they supported the charges with a number of false witnesses. People soon began to notice a change in his attitude, and he became much cooler towards King Hrolf than he'd been before. King Hrolf paid no attention, and so time went by.

One day the two earls came to see King Ælla and repeated the charges of treason. The King said, 'Since you think he's guilty of treason against us, you've my permission to give him the punishment he deserves. But he's a guest in my house, and he hasn't been openly treacherous, so whatever you plan to do, I'll keep out of it.'

The King put it this way because he suspected them of lying to him; and the earls said they wouldn't ask for anything more of the King than this. Then they fixed the time to attack King Hrolf, deciding to go for him with weapons and fire. The King told them they could do as they pleased. In the evening when the earls were due to come, King Ælla had the drinks served very generously and made himself very friendly towards King Hrolf. Most of the men got very drunk. But when others got drunk, that was when King Hrolf used to drink least. He slept in a separate house and used to go to bed early, and that's what he did on this occasion.

King Ælla said, 'You've been a guest in our land for some time now, and we've always admired the good manners you and your men have, and how well-bred you are and courtly all the time. I'd like to sleep in your house tonight to see if your men conduct themselves as well by night as by day.'

King Hrolf said, 'You're more than welcome, and if you're willing to be so humble, we'll be happy to welcome you.'

When the tables had been taken away, King Ælla went with King Hrolf over to his sleeping-quarters. They lay down and were soon fast asleep.

Shortly afterwards, King Hrolf was woken by a loud din of shouting and the clash of weapons from outside. Then the house was set on fire. King Hrolf told his men to get up and take their weapons. 'This is a terrible mischance for King Ælla to be spending the night in peril here, just because these men have some grudge against us, and it's a disgrace for a good and honest king to have to suffer because of us.'

King Hrolf tried to wake the King, but he couldn't. He was so fast asleep he didn't hear all the noise.

King Hrolf said, 'We'd better make a quick decision before the house is burnt down round us. We'll take the bench-boards, ram them against the timber wall, and break through.'

He chose the strongest men there, told them to lift King Ælla as he was, fully dressed, and carry him over to his own bedroom. 'Be very careful with the King whatever you do, our honour depends on it,' he said.

When they got outside, they saw a large crowd there, and right away sharp fighting broke out. Once King Ælla was outside, he called out and ordered the men to stop fighting. Then he told King Hrolf what had happened, and said this had been partly his doing. He asked King Hrolf to forgive him for this trick, and promised to have the slanderers put to death, but King Hrolf said they shouldn't be killed just because of this, which made him extremely popular with the English.

So the two Kings stayed as close friends as ever, and King Ælla treated King Hrolf even more hospitably than before, having proved there was nobody like Hrolf when it came to loyalty. So the winter passed, and it was summer again.

CHAPTER 27

The berserk

ARLY ONE MORNING King Hrolf got out of bed and took
a long walk by himself some distance from the house. He
didn't have much on in the way of clothes, but he never went
anywhere night or day without having the giant's sword with
him. The King took a look around, and just as he was about to
walk back to his sleeping quarters, he saw a big man riding very
hard. He was well armed, not very tall, and yet a lively sort of
man. When he saw the King standing there, he turned towards
him, dismounted, and greeted him politely. The King gave him
a friendly reply, and asked who he was. He said his name was
Thord and he owned property further inland. The King asked
him where he was going.

'No further, now that I've found you,' said Thord.

'What do you want with me?' the King asked.

'I'm in a bit of a quandary,' he replied. 'Three years ago a man
called Harek came to see me, if you could call him a man, for
he's more like a troll. He's a dangerous berserk and utterly
ruthless. I've a sister called Gyda, a fine woman, and this man
Harek wanted to take her for his concubine, but I refused. So
he challenged me to a duel, and I accepted it. Now I realise I'm
no match for this giant. I've heard about all the great things
you've done, and now I'm asking you to save me from this
threat and kill the berserk.'

'You've got a problem on your hands,' said the King, 'and

I'd like to meet this fellow. I'm going back to my quarters to get my clothes and weapons.'

Thord said, 'You can't do that, you'll have to come as you are. I'm afraid the berserk's already arrived, and he'll think I'm too much of a coward to wait for him, and then he'll carry off my sister. So mount this horse, my lord, and take these clothes and weapons.'

Thord had them ready for him and kept dancing attendance on him. So the King mounted the horse and rode off, with Thord running in front. All this was taking place well inland.

When they came to Thord's farm, Harek hadn't arrived. The King could see the farm was a fine one. They went inside into the living-room, where a high-seat had been made ready for him, and there were plenty of people in the household. The King thought Gyda a really attractive woman. After they'd been waiting a while, Harek arrived with eleven others, all arrogant men, and they asked if Thord was ready for the duel.

He said, 'I've got someone else to fight on my behalf, as our agreement allows.'

Harek asked who was so bold as to offer to fight him, and Thord told him it was King Hrolf Gautreksson.

Harek said, 'I've heard about King Hrolf. There aren't many kings nowadays who approach him for courage and skill and all kinds of talents. Anyway, it's much more fitting for me to be up against him, I think it beneath my dignity to fight you. So up you get, King Hrolf, if you're willing to risk your reputation against my weapons.'

The King said he thought fighting Harek wasn't much of a

risk, and then they went outside. A cloak was spread under their feet, and the berserk recited the rules of combat. The King had no weapon except the giant's sword. Thord held the shield for the King, and with the first blow the King split the berserk's head right through to the shoulders and he dropped straight down dead. Thord thanked the King for winning and gave him magnificent gifts, for he was very rich. The King asked him not to marry off his sister until he came back from Ireland, if that was to be, and Thord gave his promise.

After that he saw the King home, and as they arrived back in town they heard a great deal of noise. Asmund had woken up shortly after the King had left and had started searching for him all over town. He wasn't in the best of moods, but when the King got back safely everybody was glad to see him. King Ælla asked him where he'd been and King Hrolf told him exactly what had happened. King Ælla said he'd had good luck to beat the worst berserk pestering England, robbing and tyrannising over everybody, and he thanked King Hrolf warmly for what he'd done. King Hrolf put an end to plenty more crimes that winter, and travelled widely through England with King Ælla. He helped settle many a judgement for King Ælla, who was getting on in years by then. King Hrolf became very popular all over England, and whenever he wanted anything done, everybody sprang to do it.

Iron-Shield goes to Ireland

N OW WE TAKE UP the story where we left off, with Queen
Thornbjorg in Sweden. She'd had no news of King Hrolf's
travels, and after he'd been twelve months out of the country
she began to get very worried about the expedition.

The story goes that Thorir Iron-Shield was sitting in the
high-seat, as he usually did, with only a small group of men
around him. The Queen came into the hall, carrying the famous
drinking-horn, and went up to Thorir. She offered him a drink
and said he must be very thirsty. Thorir was surprised the horn
should be brought into the hall, because he hadn't seen it since
King Hrolf's departure. Another thing that baffled him was why
the Queen herself should be serving him drinks, for she'd
never done that before. Thorir had vowed before King Hrolf
left Sweden that he'd kill the man who brought him the news of
King Hrolf's death. Thorir got to his feet, greeted the Queen
warmly, took the horn from her and started drinking from it.
When he'd nearly emptied it, the horn gave out a loud noise,
as it usually did before or after events of great importance such
as major battles or the deaths of great men.

Thorir Iron-Shield flung the horn away and looked at the
Queen angrily. 'Are you telling me King Hrolf Gautreksson's
been killed?'

'No, I'm not,' she said, 'but I can hear the horn's telling you
some great news, whether it's happened already or is about to

happen. I've had dreams warning me that King Hrolf will be needing more men before this summer's over.'

'Now that you've told me what's worrying you, my lady, that you're troubled about King Hrolf, and since I owe him such a great debt, as you know, I'm going to leave this country and not come back till I find out what's happened to him, and whether he's alive or dead. I won't be able to eat or drink till I know how matters stand with him and exactly what he's doing.'

Then he got a small boat and sailed away from Sweden with only a few men. When he reached England, King Hrolf had already left for Ireland. Thorir wasted no time there, for he was anxious to help King Hrolf, and didn't stop till he reached Ireland, though at a different spot from Hrolf's landing-place.

Thorir said to his men, 'Wait for me here. I'm going ashore by myself. I can't tell you when to expect me back, but don't ever mention my name even, though you may be tempted to ask about my movements. It may be I'll do something that won't make you altogether popular with the people here. Say that you're merchants, and stay here quietly till I come back.'

With that Thorir left the ship under cover of darkness. He travelled far inland and didn't reveal himself to anyone. He made his way towards the King's residence, and as soon as he thought no-one would suspect the reason for his journey, he started killing men and cattle. Everyone who saw him thought a dangerous troll had turned up, and all those who could made a run for it, offering no resistance.

CHAPTER 29

In an Irish prison

NEXT WE TAKE UP the story of King Hrolf again. Early in the spring he'd called his men together and got ready for the voyage to Ireland. King Ælla offered him as many men as he wanted. King Hrolf left his dragon-ship behind, as well as the biggest ships, but took a number of smaller ones with him and sailed from England with a fleet of thirty small ships. Grim came and joined him as they'd agreed. The two Kings parted the best of friends; and, when everything was ready, King Hrolf set out from England. They'd favourable winds, reaching Ireland late one evening, and there they spent the night.

The story goes that King Hrolf of Ireland knew beforehand all about his namesake's arrival through his witchcraft and magic, and that's why he'd had a large army gathered.

In the morning, when the blood-brothers woke up, King Hrolf said to Asmund, 'Wouldn't it be a good idea to get on with this marriage proposal and hear what King Hrolf has to say about it?'

Asmund said that was just what he wanted.

The King said, 'We must go about this peaceably and not make any show of force or violence as long as nobody threatens us.'

The King picked a hundred men to come with him, and told the rest of the troops to leave the ships, go into the forest near the town, and keep themselves ready for battle should they be needed. Hrolf set out and as they approached the town, they saw an army in full battle coming towards them. The King told his men to march on, and the two armies began to close. Eventually they met, and it turned out to be the King of Ireland with six hundred men.

King Hrolf of Ireland said, 'I know very well who you are, Hrolf Gautreksson, and your blood-brother too, Asmund, son of King Olaf of Scotland. I know why you've come as well, so there's no need for you to state your business. I'm giving you a quick choice, King Hrolf. Since you're the most handsome and famous of kings, I'll give you leave to go back home with all your men unharmed. But never come here again on the same business. Better men than you, and more famous, have come with the same idea in mind and got nothing but shame and humiliation. If you won't accept this offer, you'll only be humbled all the more for thinking so much more highly of yourself than of any other man.'

When King Hrolf of Ireland had finished his speech, King Hrolf Gautreksson replied to him. 'Since you've so much wisdom and foresight that you know what's going to happen and what everyone's thinking and wanting, it seems sensible to accept your offer. On the other hand, I've travelled all the way from Sweden with these men and promised my blood-brother Asmund my loyal support in this matter, and I'm not turning back now without putting your strength and power to some test.'

The King of Ireland told him he'd made the worst possible choice for himself and his men. King Hrolf sent word to his men to hurry up and help him. He thought the Irish King only had the troops they could see, and that it would be a child's play for him to win. Now, while the Irish King had an immense army the others didn't know about, he knew nothing about the troops King Hrolf Gautreksson was keeping in the forest. The Irish King ordered his men to attack, while King Hrolf Gautreksson told his to look out for themselves and fall back. Soon afterwards more troops came up to join the Irish King, but he told them to retreat to the town. A number of the Irish were killed before they got inside, and Hrolf's men followed hard on their heels right into the town.

When Hrolf's whole army was inside the town walls, they were attacked on all sides, and both armies dug in their heels. People say the Swedes were outnumbered six to one. This put a good many of them into a panic, they thought such a great mass of men too much to fight against. The battle was long and hard, and large numbers of the Irish kept attacking the Swedes, because they knew what a great killer their own leader was. The Irish King was shooting so fast there seemed always to be two arrows coming from him, and every one of them took a man's life. King Hrolf Gautreksson put up a good fight. All his men gave him staunch and loyal support, and died bravely, and though we can't record the comings and goings of each and every one, it was clear that many of them were magnificent fighters. As long as they could stand, they cut down man after man, and didn't give an inch in spite of the heavy odds against them.

The man Grim we spoke about earlier was outstanding in the battle, a brave, lithe, and fast-moving fighter. King Hrolf Gautreksson fought hard, hewing to left and right with the

127

giant's sword, without helmet or shield or mailcoat to protect himself, and sent a good many men to their deaths as he hacked a brave path through the enemy. Asmund, too, battled on, striking hard and fast in defence and creating havoc around him.

The battle grew fiercer with the greatest slaughter on both sides, but, as so often happens, it was the home army that won the day. King Hrolf Gautreksson's men began suffering the heavier losses, and when the Irish saw the way the battle was going their fighting hearts rose. So King Hrolf Gautreksson's men began to fall piled one on top of the other as the Irish came at them screaming and howling from every side.

When King Hrolf saw his men going down and only few left standing, he told the survivors to fall back towards the town wall for shelter. They said they wanted to make a run for it, hoping to get back to the ships, but the King said he'd no intention of running, he'd rather die with his men. The outcome was that no-one ran, and so one after another they died, until there were only twelve of them left, and they were badly hurt and completely worn out.

Then King Hrolf said to Asmund, 'It seems you'll have to earn the place you were so keen to get in the Irish King's family circle. You thought I was too slow and hesitant about this mission. Well, now I've made up my mind to do all I can to help you get the girl and the dowry.'

King Hrolf Gautreksson took the sword-handle with both hands and hit out right and left with swift, hard strokes, giving many a man a quick death. Asmund and Grim followed him close. It's said they piled the corpses so high around themselves they could hardly fight, and in the end none of them were left alive except for King Hrolf, Asmund and Grim, and they were so badly wounded they could barely stand.

Then shields crowded in on them from all sides, though before they were captured, King Hrolf Gautreksson killed fifteen of the enemy. The old saying was borne out again, "Numbers always tell", and they were taken prisoner and stripped of their clothes and weapons. Hrolf's men had been fighting all day and most of the night, and now they were all dead, without a single survivor. They'd wanted nothing but to do their best to help their King like good retainers. The King of Ireland had lost so many of his troops that only five hundred men were left, every one of them wounded and worn out.

King Hrolf of Ireland boasted of his victory to King Hrolf Gautreksson: 'Now it's turned out just as I expected, you and your men are finished. You'd have been better off if you'd accepted my offer in the right spirit and saved your men's lives.'

King Hrolf Gautreksson said, 'You don't deserve any credit for it. As for that mob you brought against us, you've won the victory with sharp practice, not brave hearts, and the time may still come when you'll be paid back for this.'

The King of the Irish said, 'You still keep on fooling yourself, but wait till you see what lies ahead. You're going into the foulest place in town.'

King Hrolf Gautreksson said, 'You've got us for the time being. But isn't it the normal custom to behead good fighting-men?'

'I'd rather have you taken to my guest-room to starve to death,' said the Irish King.

He had them led out to the courtyard, where they saw a pit plunging deep into the earth. It took a good many men to force King Hrolf into the pit. It was so deep the King would have died if they'd thrown him in head first, but he landed on his feet. There was an ugly stench down there, with decaying corpses lying about. Asmund and Grim were thrown down beside him, and a huge slab was placed over the opening, too heavy for ten men to budge.

Then the men of Ireland went off to take things easy.

CHAPTER 30

The Irish princess

KING HROLF GAUTREKSSON said to Asmund, 'Well, blood-brother, it seems that my namesake would rather you slept here than next to his daughter Ingibjorg. What do you make of the hospitality?'

Asmund said he didn't like it a bit. 'I'd rather have been slaughtered by brave men's swords today than end up like this. We must be meant to starve to death here.'

King Hrolf said, 'Let's talk like men, foster-brother. As the saying goes, "Strange things laed to better," and there's bound to be something good round the corner.'

130

They were standing in shirt sleeves and linen pants, barefoot, on human corpses.

The daughter of the King of Ireland had been watching the battle all day and admiring the brave fight King Hrolf Gautreksson had been putting up, along with his men. She was far from happy that the life of such an outstanding king should have to be cut short like that. She had a boudoir where she lived with a number of girls. She was shrewd and well-liked, very courteous and good-looking. She had a boudoir-maid called Sigrid she trusted better than all the others, the daughter of an important man in Ireland.

When the battle was over, the Princess called the girl to her and said, 'Go over to the pit where King Hrolf Gautreksson and his men are held captive and ask him what he would like me to do for him most, if I could.'

The girl went over to the pit and asked whether anyone was still alive there. The King said three of them were.

The girl said, 'The daughter of the King of Ireland told me to ask you, King Hrolf Gautreksson, what she could do to help you.'

The King said, 'I can tell you that. Most of all I'd want her to get my sword for me. She can't miss it on the battlefield, because of its size and shape. When I was captured, I took care to throw it as far as I could, right where the corpses were piled up highest.'

The girl ran back to the boudoir to tell Ingibjorg what had happened, and said the King must be a very stupid man to ask for something of no use to him in his present state.

'I've been told King Hrolf is the wisest of men.' said the Princess, 'so go and look for the sword.'

The girl said she didn't dare go and search there among the dead on the battlefield all by herself, wading through blood and treading on corpses; that wasn't the thing for ladies. The Princess ordered her to go, and said she'd come to no harm; and so at last, very frightened, as the Princess kept urging her to go, off she went. She searched for the sword and couldn't find it, so she came back and told the Princess the dead were walking about all over the place.

The Princess said she was both a coward and a fool to be afraid of dead people. 'I'll go with you,' she said.

The two of them went together to search the battlefield. The Princess went about it boldly and found the sword, and they dragged it behind them back to her boudoir.

The Princess said to the girl, 'Go back to the pit and ask King Hrolf what else he'd like me to do for him, if I could.'

The girl set out and reached the pit. She told them they'd got the sword and asked what they wanted next. The king said things were looking up.

The girl asked, 'Tell me, what would you most like?'

'What we'd most like,' replied the King, 'would be a cloth to put under our feet, because it's cold and foul standing on these corpses. I see there's a gap under the slab in one place where you can get stuff through.'

The girl went back to the Princess and told her what they wanted. Ingibjorg said, 'King Hrolf keeps showing how much braver and stronger he is than any other king. Lots of people would have been much more impatient about their chances of getting rescued if they were in his place. It's a terrible thing that such brave men should soon have to die.'

She got all the things they needed most, food and drink, good ointments and medicine, clothes and a light, and everything else they wanted, then went with the girl and gave them all these things. They had a string and lowered the stuff down to them, and in the same way they brought them King Hrolf's sword. He was very relieved and couldn't thank them enough. Then he took a look at the wounds on Asmund and Grim and saw none of them was deadly. So they made themselves comfortable, put on the clothes and ate and drank. They thought things were looking better but they still had a lot to put up with.

CHAPTER 31

Expedition

NEXT WE COME to events in Sweden, Denmark, and Gotaland. Thorir Iron-Shield was in charge of the kingdom of Sweden after King Hrolf had gone, as we've mentioned already. Ingjald and Ketil were very unhappy that they'd been left behind, and after Thorir set out from Sweden Queen Thornbjorg sent word to them to gather forces and look for King Hrolf Gautreksson. They wasted no time and ordered a levy in Denmark and Gotaland.

The Queen mustered an army in Sweden, took her shield and

sword, and set out with her son Gautrek who was twelve years
old at the time, an extremely handsome lad, big and strong. All
the leaders met with large forces at the appointed place with the
Queen in charge commanding the whole army. On this occasion
as usual, Ketil showed more determination than foresight or
judgement, and wanted everything on this expedition to happen
at once. But now we have to leave them to get on with their
journey as they please.

CHAPTER 32

The giant

AFTER HE'D DISCOVERED, by means of his witchcraft, that
King Hrolf Gautreksson was on his way, King Hrolf of
Ireland, as we know, had gathered his forces. One day, after
he'd kept his men together for a fortnight, this monstrous giant
turned up in Ireland near the royal residence. This giant was so
savage and ruthless that nothing could stop him, he went about
killing men and beasts, burning down settlements, and not
sparing a thing. He killed every living creature and caused a
vast amount of damage, and the few survivors fled into woods
and forests. This giant came to the town the morning after the
battle between the Kings. King Hrolf of Ireland had spent
most of the night drinking, after which he and all his men had
gone to sleep.

In the morning when the retainers wanted to go out, there was this giant, so huge they'd never seen anything like him, blocking the palace door. The giant was fully armed and carrying a great iron-lined shield which covered the entire door, and he looked so savage and frightening that no-one dared go outside. He struck such terror into everyone there that the King lost all his wisdom and cunning and was more scared than anyone by what was going on. Everybody thought it a terror and a wonder that such an amazing thing should happen there. The giant behaved as if he was going to rush into the hall at any moment and set on them. The king told his men no-one must dare attack the giant, and maybe he would soon go away. They had to spend the whole day under the shadow of this giant, and didn't think it at all amusing.

CHAPTER 33

Rescue

THE PRINCESS'S HANDMAID went to the hall that day and as she got near she saw the huge giant there at the hall, and ran back to the boudoir screaming in a panic. The Princess asked why she was behaving so stupidly.

She said there was a giant standing in the door of the hall. 'He's so huge, there's nothing like him.'

The Princess asked, 'Are you sure this is a giant, not a man?'

'There can't be another giant like this one,' she said, 'and he looks so savage he'll spare nothing if he gets the chance.'

The Princess said, 'This isn't a giant, though he may behave like one. But I think it's likely he'll be in a savage temper and looking for revenge. I want you to go over to the palace, and take food with you to offer the giant. There may be a chance that he's not so savage after all and he may be friendlier when he meets someone.'

'What you're saying is ridiculous,' said the handmaid, 'to ask a young girl like me to go against this giant, when the King himself, your father, is too frightened to go outside, and he's a great champion. The same's true of all his men, they'd rather starve to death. You're very keen to give food to the one who wants to kill the King, your father. I think you've been bewitched by this monster that's marching about here in broad daylight.'

But though she kept talking like that, she didn't dare go against the wishes of the Princess. She carried a plate on the palm of her hand, and in the other she held a great drinking-horn. When she came close enough for him to hear her, she shouted out, 'Eat your food, giant.'

He looked at her, and she was so scared she ran screaming back to the boudoir, spilling the food from the plate and the drink from the horn. She said it was ridiculous to put her in the hands of giants.

'Do you want to kill me?' she asked.

The Princess said she didn't want the girl to be killed or come to any harm because of her orders. 'Nothing's going to happen to you. I've got a feeling this isn't a giant at all. You'd better go again.'

The girl went once more, very much against her will, and

when she came close enough to see the giant clearly, she said, 'Would you like to take some food, great giant?'

He stared at her and made faces and she ran off to tell the Princess she'd taken a good look at the giant.

The Princess said, 'What do you think of the giant? Did he talk to you at all?'

'I've never seen a giant before,' she said, 'but I didn't think he's so much evil-looking as just huge. He's lean and hungry, and must have been starving for a long time. I'm surprised he's not eating up all the corpses littering the town. Perhaps he's only a half-giant and not a full-blooded one, I wasn't as frightened this time as I was before.'

'How's the giant dressed?' asked the Princess.

'He's wearing an enormous fur cloak,' she replied, 'so big it covers his feet and hands. He's carrying a shield that blocks the entire door of the hall, and a horrible spear he keeps pushing into the hall on one side of the shield.'

'I'll tell you what to do,' said the Princess, 'go to the giant again, offer him the food and tell him King Hrolf Gautreksson's alive. See what happens then.'

The girl plucked up the courage she didn't have before. When she got close to him, she stretched out her hand with the plate, and said, 'Eat your food, big giant. Hrolf Gautreksson's alive.'

He gave her a friendly look, took the plate from her, and started eating and drinking. She saw he had a raging appetite for the food, yet he didn't eat like a slave. When he'd had enough, she went away. The night was wearing on. She told the Princess what had happened and how he'd taken the food.

'Under the cloak I could see a red sleeve and there was a gold bracelet on his arm,' she said.

The night passed, and the people in the hall had no idea of how to cope with this giant and couldn't get out. In the morning when the girl came back again with food for him, he grabbed her by the hand and sat her on his knee and she started screaming.

He told her not to be afraid. 'Tell me where King Hrolf Gautreksson is and who saved his life.'

She spoke up and told him everything that had happened on the expedition, and how things stood.

He said, 'Tell the Princess I'm coming to see her tonight. I'd like to have a talk with her.'

Then he let her go and she ran back to the boudoir to tell the Princess how the giant had grabbed her and had quite a lot to say to her. 'He's coming to see you tonight.'

The Princess said it was a good idea, and that this was a man she needn't be afraid of.

He came to the boudoir that night, and the story goes that the Princess wasn't in the least put out when she saw this giant. They started talking and she asked him what he planned to do.

He said all he wanted to do was to starve the King and his men to death in the hall. 'But since King Hrolf Gautreksson's still alive and you were the one to save him, I'll do anything you say.'

'I can think of better things,' she said, 'than to have my father starved to death like a fox in a hole or a vixen in her den. I've had dreams warning me there's going to be more fighting soon,

138

and I think it won't be long before King Hrolf Gautreksson starts getting reinforcements.'

'All I want is to see my foster-son,' said Thorir.

She said she could easily fix it for them to have a talk, but that it was impossible to get them out of the pit without a great number of men.

They went over to the pit, and when Thorir saw the slab they were trapped behind, he seized it with all his strength and hurled it into a field yards away. Then he lowered a rope into the pit and hauled them up. This was a happy reunion between them, and each felt he was reclaiming the other from the dead. Then they all went to the boudoir where they started drinking and enjoying themselves. King Hrolf asked what they should do next.

Asmund said that was easily settled. 'The first thing to do is to set fire to the hall and burn the king and all his men inside it.'

The Princess came up to them and said, 'King Hrolf, I'd like to ask you to spare the life of my father if you get him in your power.'

The King said he'd gladly do as she wished because she'd been so virtuous and ladylike in giving him help and he added that a favour from him was what she deserved.

CHAPTER 34
Queen Thornbjorg's expedition

NEXT WE'D BETTER TELL how Queen Thornbjorg and the Kings, Ketil and Ingjald were getting on with their expedition. They fitted out their forces and took sixty ships with them, all big and manned with good crews. They had an easy voyage and reached Ireland on the very night King Hrolf was rescued from the prison where he'd been put by King Hrolf of Ireland with the prospect of suffering a miserable death. But now the Irish King and his men didn't dare to go outside because of the huge giant. When Ketil and the others arrived, they saw a large fleet and recognised many of the ships as belonging to King Hrolf Gautreksson. The ships were all deserted, which came as a great shock to them as they realised what must have happened. They made a determined rush towards the hall with a great deal of noise and soon saw the proofs of what had happened. This distressed a good many of them. Queen Thornbjorg asked what they should do next.

Ketil said, 'Follow my advice, set fire to every house and hamlet and burn to cinders everything that comes our way.'

'That's not my idea,' said the Queen. 'We've plenty of men to deal with them, because there aren't many of their troops left – King Hrolf and his men must have seen to that before he was killed. But it could be that they're staying in some house or other, and we don't want to harm them any more than we do

ourselves. I can see the town's not been cleared yet of the bodies
of those killed in this battle.'

But Ketil insisted on having things his way, so they got some
fire and set every house ablaze.

CHAPTER 35

Voyage from Ireland

THE STORY GOES that King Hrolf Gautreksson and his
companions were drinking and having a good time when
they heard a loud din and the clash of weapons outside, and
next moment, the boudoir where they were enjoying themselves
was set on fire. As it happened, Queen Thornbjorg herself and
her son Gautrek were in charge of this part of the army.

'It seems to me, Thorir my friend,' said King Hrolf, 'that your
shield's not offered much protection against the King's men.
They must have all got out. So we'd better let them get the feel
of our weapons before they finish us off.'

They jumped to their feet and armed themselves. Then the
Princess said, 'As soon as you get outside, sir, you'll see these
aren't the men of the King of Ireland, but your friends and
kinsmen. Remember what you promised me, now.'

They grabbed a log and rammed and smashed the door, and
so broke out. At once King Hrolf saw that the men there were
Swedes and Gotalanders. Facing him stood a man, fully armed
and very warlike. This man lifted his helmet and pushed it

on to the back of his head, and then King Hrolf realised it was
Queen Thornbjorg.

The King said, 'It takes a long time to tame a woman like
you: now you're trying to suffocate me here like a fox in its lair.'

'There are better ways of looking at it, my lord,' she said, 'if
you really want to. We're not doing this out of malice. Now we
can rejoice over a complete victory since you who matter most
are all safe and sound. So let's do what's best for all of us.'

King Hrolf ordered them to put out the fires at once. Soon the
word spread among all the troops that King Hrolf was safe and
unhurt, and Asmund and Thorir Iron-Shield too, which was
cheering news to all the leading men and the troops in general.
It was an easy matter to put out the fires as they'd only been lit
in a few places.

When the King of Ireland saw that fighting had begun and
that the giant wasn't in the door of the hall any longer, he broke
out with his men, and they put up a stout defence of the hall.
King Ketil was there, attacking them with fire and steel, and
there was some loss of life before King Hrolf came on the scene
and told them to put out the fires. Then he attacked with all
his strength and determination, and had King Hrolf of Ireland
taken prisoner, and everyone killed who tried to stand in his way.

When this was done, King Hrolf Gautreksson said, 'Now this
is how things stand, namesake, that you were in a position to
kill me a couple of nights ago, and would have put me to a cruel
death had our situation not taken a turn for the better. But now
everything's changed, because I've got you and your whole
future in my hands, and you'll have to accept my terms. Are

you willing now to take my blood-brother Asmund, son of the King of the Scots, as your son-in-law, and in return be given your life and the lives of your men along with peace and freedom?'

King Hrolf of Ireland said he agreed to these terms. King Ketil Gautreksson and the other allies thought it odd that King Hrolf of Ireland wasn't put to death right away, considering all the damage he'd done to their army. They'd lost many a good warrior and nobleman. But King Hrolf Gautreksson said he was doing this mostly for the Princess because she'd been so helpful to him and his companions, though King Hrolf of Ireland deserved nothing good from them. He said the Irish King was evil, full of foul tricks, and that it was mostly thanks to his friend Thorir Iron-Shield that Hrolf hadn't been able to do the damage with his sorcery that he usually did, but had suffered instead the shame and humiliation he deserved.

Then the King of Ireland gave his daughter a great deal of money in gold and silver and all kinds of treasures, because they wanted to get away from Ireland as quickly as they could and wouldn't grant the King of Ireland the honour of celebrating his daughter's wedding. They treated him as roughly as they could, short of killing him, taking his wealth from him without a word of thanks. Then they sailed away from Ireland with all the ships they could get and a great deal of money. The troops were in a very cheerful mood, having got back their King and the other leaders they loved so dearly, and gained this clever good-looking bride Ingibjorg too, and all the men she chose to take with her.

They landed in England where King Ælla gave a good welcome to King Hrolf Gautreksson and took the casualties his own men had suffered in good part. Then they sent the whole army back home under the leadership of three commanders. One was a Dane called Aki, another was a Gotalander called Bjorn, and the third, of Swedish stock, was called Brynjolf. These were men of importance who were to take charge of the defences and run the three kingdoms until the Kings came back home. The Kings kept twelve well-manned ships, and stayed in England for a long time.

King Hrolf arranged a marriage between Grim Thorkelsson and Gyda, the sister of Thord who was mentioned earlier. Grim wanted to go with King Hrolf and never part from him. King Ælla asked King Hrolf to leave Thorir Iron-Shield in England to defend the realm and strengthen his kingdom, and since Thorir was willing, that's what happened. King Hrolf did this to please King Ælla, and Thorir married Sigrid, the handmaid who'd served Princess Ingibjorg. She was the daughter of a man of note in Ireland and was considered a fine match. Thorir became a great man in England, and everybody always thought him a splendid champion and very brave, but we can't say much about his journey through Ireland or about whether he kept his vow or not. People can often live a long time on things that aren't food, strictly speaking, such as different herbs and roots. He and King Hrolf parted the best of friends, and now Thorir's out of the story.

CHAPTER 36

Back home

AFTER THAT, KING HROLF got ready to leave England. He and King Ælla parted the best of friends, and King Hrolf sailed towards Scotland. When King Olaf heard that King Hrolf, his son, and the rest of the blood-brothers had arrived, he prepared a magnificent feast for them, and invited King Hrolf with all his men. The King himself went out to meet them and gave them a warm friendly welcome. On the advice of King Hrolf, King Ingjald spoke up and asked for the hand of Olaf's daughter, and since Asmund offered his support too, the King gave a favourable answer. A splendid feast was prepared, where the two bridegrooms celebrated their weddings, Ingjald to Margaret, daughter of the King of Scotland, and Asmund to Ingibjorg, daughter of the King of Ireland; after the feast King Hrolf got lodgings for his men in Scotland, but the Kings stayed with King Olaf in honour and splendour, every one of them very well contented.

During the winter King Olaf of Scotland died; he was getting on in years, and had been a distinguished ruler. Then Asmund took charge of the kingdom of Scotland, ruling extremely capably and popular with everyone. The following summer the Kings got their ships ready, but Asmund stayed behind. He offered to let Gautrek, King Hrolf's son, stay with him, and with his father's approval Gautrek accepted the offer, and stayed with King Asmund for a long time. Asmund gave him ships, and he set off on viking expeditions and became a very famous man. We've been told he harried in Ireland with the help of King Asmund, and claimed the kingdom there from Hrolf of Ireland. Asmund thought this should have been his, since Ingibjorg was the only daughter of the King of Ireland; all the same, because of his friendship with King Hrolf Gautreksson and their blood-brotherhood he didn't begrudge the kingship to Gautrek.

After this King Hrolf got ready to leave Scotland. Asmund gave him a good many splendid gifts, and they parted the best of friends, staying on good terms for the rest of their lives. King Hrolf arrived back home in Sweden, and everybody was delighted to see and welcome their lord. Ketil and Ingjald spent only a short time in Sweden, then Ingjald went back home to Denmark and Ketil to Gotaland. King Hrolf gave up most of his military affairs and stayed at home for a while. His son Eirik grew up there, and became a man extraordinary for his size, good-looks and talents of every kind. When Eirik was fully grown, King Hrolf gave him ships, and Gautrek got the dragon-ship that had been Grimar's with all the military equipment that had belonged to King Hrolf, his father. Gautrek set out on viking expeditions with strong forces and a hard mind, and became a man of outstanding fame and widespread reputation.

CHAPTER 37

The saga ends

THEN OVER IN RUSSIA King Halfdan died, and on his death the kingdom passed to rulers who had no claim to it. When King Hrolf and his brother Ketil heard this, they went over there, threw the usurpers out, killing some of them, and then pacified and liberated the whole kingdom. Ketil became king over it, and gained more of a reputation for his courage, ambition, arrogance, and enthusiasm than for his wisdom and wit. All the same, he was popular and had plenty of support from his brother Hrolf. Then King Hrolf took charge of Gotaland and often resided there. Grim Thorkelsson kept up his friendship with King Hrolf.

King Hrolf carried on ruling over Sweden, and people thought him the greatest of all kings because of his ability and open-handedness, traits he'd inherited from his father. No king dared to attack his land. He became the strongest of rulers, and plenty of people looked to him for friendship, expecting to derive peace and freedom from his strength, instead of the war and oppression many others had to suffer from. No-one would dare attack him. King Hrolf lived to be an old man, and died in his bed. King Eirik inherited the kingdom and reigned over all the lands his father had ruled. He became a king of some reputation and was very much like his father.

PEOPLE SAY this is a true story. Although it's never been
committed to vellum, learned men have preserved it in their
memories with many of King Hrolf's exploits not recorded
here – a slow pen would be exhausted sooner than his great
deeds. The same applies to this story as to a good many others,
that people tell it differently. But there are all kinds of people,
some travel more widely than others, one man gets to hear what
another doesn't, and both may be telling the truth even though
neither knows the whole truth. It shouldn't surprise anyone
that people used to be bigger and stronger than they are now,
because it looks as if their claim to be descended from the giants
could be true, and not so very far back either. But now people
are levelling out as the races get mixed. It's likely that a lot of
small men would have been killed by the strokes of the big ones,
since weapons those days were so heavy that the weaker sort
could hardly have been able to lift them from the ground.
It's obvious that small men wouldn't be likely to survive being
hit with such strong blows and sharp edges. Even if the weapons
failed to bite, anything in their way would be badly damaged,
and I think you shouldn't find fault with the story unless you
can improve on it. But whether it's true or not, let those enjoy
the story who can, while those who can't had better look for
some other amusement.

AND SO WE COME TO THE END
OF THE STORY OF
KING HROLF
GAUTREKS-
SON
✳